Advance I

Live Your Happiest is a delightful, heartfelt, illuminating journey to the heart of healing. Maria Felipes sincerity shines as a light to illuminate the path to soul fulfillment we all share. Her stories ring of authenticity and the wisdom gained from experience. She writes with extraordinary clarity and ability to touch readers where we live. If you are seeking miracles and deep well-being in your life, applying the profound truths in this precious book will accelerate your journey home.
— ALAN COHEN, author of *Of Course in Miracles*

With her new book, Rev. Maria Felipe gives us a very helpful explanation of how profound spiritual principles, including a new, advanced form of forgiveness, can go a long way toward eliminating suffering from your daily experience. Maria is not only a long-time close friend of mine, but I've seen her in person brilliantly answering people's most difficult questions about life and their relationships. Don't miss this opportunity to get a crash course in happiness from one of the most important spiritual teachers and authors working today.
— GARY R. RENARD, best-selling author of *The Disappearance of the Universe* trilogy and *The Lifetimes When Jesus and Buddha Knew Each Other.*

If you want to simplify and enhance your path to peace with enthusiasm, dedication and authenticity, this book will inspire you! A compassionate teacher who is honestly walking this path, Maria truly wants to help you "challenge the thoughts" that cause pain and suffering. Maria's writing is infused with positive energy, guiding the reader with personal examples, humor, and a formula for addressing any situation or problem. Get ready to embrace your inner happiness in a permanent way! — JACKIE LORA-JONES, author of *All Peace No Pieces: A Course in Miracles' Take on "the World"*

As a fellow teacher of *A Course in Miracles* and someone who's known Maria for years, I can say this book is a must-read! With heartfelt stories, practical tools, and the wisdom of A Course in Miracles, Maria has created a spiritual smoothie of insights, humor, and heart. If you're ready to kick suffering to the curb and embrace joy, this book is your backstage pass to miracles and happiness. Don't just read it; live it!
 — EARL PURDY, teacher and Llcturer on *A Course in Miracles* and Metaphysics

Rev. Maria Felipe writes with purity and authenticity, bringing the light of truth forward with great transparency. I highly recommend any book written by Maria, as her work leaves the reader with practical applications, and a greater sense of purpose, peace, and joy that transcends this world.
 — CINDY LORA-RENARD, teacher and best-selling author of four books based on *A Course in Miracles*, including *Spiritual Coupling: A Guidebook for Experiencing a Holy Relationship*

Once again, Maria has thrown her heart and soul into sharing wise gems that can be truly helpful to anyone desiring to discover — and transform — the limiting beliefs and their underlying feelings and emotions that restrict our divine essence from truly being liberated into a realized, genuinely happy, life! Why wait? Dive in! — JAYEM (*Way of Mastery*)

I met Maria in April of 2016 at a Course in Miracles Conference in Las Vegas, where we were both speaking. It was pre-B3 — before the baby, book, and boyfriend — and what happened in Vegas did not stay in Vegas. We became fast friends, and I've had the incredible privilege of sitting courtside to witness her beautiful life unfold. Maria is a radiant source of spiritual wisdom and unapologetic joy. Her work is a testament to her gift for weaving profound spiritual insights with practical, transformative guidance. *Live Your Happiest* is not just a book — it's a loving, powerful invitation to live a life of true freedom, abundant joy, and deep purpose. I know that her writing will bless you, providing the tools to bless yourself and, in turn, to bless others.
—MAUREEN MULDOON, founder of Miracles LIVE 365, SpeakEasy Spiritual Community, and author of *The Spiritual Vixen's Guide to an Unapologetic Life*

Maria's new book lives up to its title. It is indeed a practical guide to "living your happiest." Personal examples and inspired practices lead the way to true forgiveness. The personal struggles she shares demonstrate the blessings that come with true forgiveness. Her successes with releasing deep perceived pain will inspire you to apply the powerful tools she offers in your own life. This book will help you make happiness and peace of mind a daily experience. — ROBERT & MARY STOELTING, Co-founders of Pathways of Light

Live Your Happiest is a heartfelt guide offering practical strategies to cultivate joy, resilience, and fulfillment in everyday life. With warmth and honesty, Maria Felipe writes like a trusted confidant, blending personal insights, actionable tips, and universal truths. The book is filled with reflection prompts, simple exercises, and motivational anecdotes to help readers embrace gratitude, nurture relationships, and find beauty in small moments. Acknowledging life's challenges, Maria emphasizes forgiveness, self-compassion, and perspective, showing that happiness is a choice we make daily. This uplifting read is a gentle reminder to cherish the present and live with greater purpose. Highly recommended!
— Eva Tamargo, Grief Counselor

Maria Felipe offers a path to happiness and healing that leads to transformation. She offers powerful examples from her own life to demonstrate the simplicity of permanently shifting the way you see yourself, the world. This book is a journey of remembering who you are and shows you how to access your true power and use it. — Lisa Natoli, founder of The Healing Cure

Live Your Happiest

A Practical Guide to Living a Suffering-Free Life!

Maria Felipe

Copyright © 2025 by Maria Felipe

First Edition published by the author in
collaboration with Fearless Literary
(www.fearlessbooks.com)
Place of Publication: Naples FL
www.mariafelipe.org

All rights reserved. This book may not be reproduced in
whole or in part, stored in a retrieval system, or transmitted in
any form or by any means — electronic, mechanical, or other
— without written permission from the publisher, except by
a reviewer, who may quote brief passages in a review.

ISBN: 979-8-9927725-0-0

Library of Congress Control Number:
2025904963

Quotations from *A Course in Miracles*,
copyright ©The Foundation for Inner Peace, are from the
Standard Third Edition, published in 2007 by The Foundation
for Inner Peace, PO Box 598, Mill Valley, CA 94942
www.acim.org

Information about The Work of Byron Katie has been
provided by Byron Katie International
www.thework.com

Cover Design: Christian Mauerer, Lovepixel Agency
www.lovepixelagency.com

TABLE OF CONTENTS

Introduction 1

Opening Prayer 6

Ch1: **You Are Forgiving Deeper** 7

Ch2: **You Are Questioning Every Thought** 19

Ch3: **You Are Free from Judgment** 33

Ch4: **You Are Embracing All of You** 47

Ch5: **You Are Healing Your Relationships** 59

Ch6: **You Are Present and Joyful** 75

Ch7: **You Are Not a Victim** 89

Ch8: **You Live Without Suffering** 101

Ch9: **You Create Lasting Change** 117

Ch10: **You Live Your Happiest** 131

Learn More with Maria Felipe 142

About the Author 144

Acknowledgments 146

Contributors 148

INTRODUCTION

WELCOME BACK, dear reader — and if you're joining me for the first time, *¡bienvenido!* This book has come to life because I want you to know that happiness is your natural inheritance — and I'm here to remind you suffering is optional. While life's challenges are inevitable, how we perceive and respond to them determines whether we remain stuck in suffering or choose the path of peace. This powerful realization is what's driven the writing of this book eight years after the release of my first, *Live Your Happy.*

Miracles Unfolding

So much has unfolded since then. In Chapter 2 of my first book I shared my ego's rant about my "big deals," namely: "Why can't I be a mom?" and "Why can't I find a partner?" Well, holy moly — I asked and the Holy Spirit answered.

In 2017, the very month that book was published, I met my husband Christian at The Happy Dream Retreat.

Within a mere six months we were engaged, married, and expecting our son Ari, who is now a smart, loving, and awesome seven-year-old. Despite having only one fallopian tube — a challenge I shared in the story of my ectopic pregnancy — I gave birth to Ari at the age of forty-one. Talk about a miracle! Meeting Christian not only fulfilled my personal dreams but also brought us together in a powerful bond of shared enthusiasm for the first book. This connection deepened as we embarked on a book tour together, further solidifying our relationship.

Since then, Christian, Ari, and I have left Los Angeles and bought our dream home in South Florida. It's been an incredible journey transitioning from the city life of Los Angeles to our peaceful haven where each day feels like a little slice of paradise.

You are here because you are ready to shift your own life in a meaningful way. This book isn't about adding more to your to-do list; it's about simplifying your path to peace, joy, and a life of greater fulfillment. Together, we'll uncover tools and practices that will empower you to live a life free from suffering and fully anchored in love.

What This Book Offers You

Now, with this book, we'll take an even deeper dive into the heart of healing and transformation. It's about understanding why we suffer, how to release the stories

INTRODUCTION 3

we tell ourselves, and how to reconnect with our true nature, which is love.

I will also unveil my new **Live Your Happy Formula** — an easy, practical way to come back to your happiest self. *¡Si!* This formula is the result of decades of trials and insights into what truly works to stop suffering in its tracks. It's designed to guide you back to joy, step by step, no matter where you are on your journey.

Since the release of my first book I've continued to deepen my understanding of *A Course in Miracles* and the tools that help us release suffering. Over the years, I've also found the work of teacher and author Byron Katie to be profoundly helpful in understanding and embodying the teachings of ACIM. Her method, known as "The Work," based on four simple yet transformative questions, has a unique way of stopping suffering in its tracks. It offers a clear path to challenge the thoughts that cause pain and return to peace. The Work perfectly complements the teachings of *A Course in Miracles*, offering a practical approach to forgiveness and freedom.

In this book, you will learn the root cause of suffering, how to heal false perceptions, and how to live in your true nature.

The answers you seek are already within you. My hope is that this book serves as a mirror to help you recognize the love and wisdom that have always been a part of you. Together, we'll remove the layers of doubt and fear, revealing the happiness that is your birthright.

This book will guide you to see that the true problem lies not in the external world but in the stories and meanings we attach to our thoughts. By addressing this inner root cause, we begin to release the blocks to love, peace, and joy that are already within us. As ACIM reminds us, "nothing outside yourself can save you; nothing outside yourself can give you peace." (ACIM, W-70.2:1). With this understanding, we'll shift from fear to love and step fully into the life of happiness we are meant to live.

An Invitation to Transform

We'll be stepping up our game, going beyond the basics to explore collective forgiveness and the nitty-gritty of personal reconciliations. I want to help boost your skills of deep emotional healing to keep the love alive and kicking.

This journey is going to rev up our understanding and acceptance, helping us to chill in the present moment and let go of judgment — because judgment kills our happy! We're stepping out of the victim zone and into our power zone, shaping our experiences with every new choice we make. It's going to be epic.

If you are holding this book, you are ready to change your life and embrace the happiness that God intends for

INTRODUCTION 5

you. And believe me, you are so worthy of this.

"You are at home in God, dreaming of exile but perfectly capable of awakening to reality." (ACIM T-10.I.2:1)

It's no accident that you are reading these words right now. In this moment, you are ready to remember your truth — to recognize how perfect everything truly is, even if it appears otherwise. You are ready for a shift in perception.

So let's embark on this happy journey together, with Spirit guiding the way. You are not alone. You are seen, you are held, and you are deeply loved, right here, right now. Let this book be a symbol that you are supported, cared for, and that all is well.

And thank you for choosing to embark on this journey with me. It's an honor to walk alongside you as we uncover the happiness that already resides within you. Together, we'll explore life-changing truths that will deepen your sense of peace and connection. Prepare for a ride filled with love, laughter, and profound transformation. *¡Vamonos!*

Opening Prayer

Dearest Holy Spirit,

As I embark on the journey of this new book, I surrender my path to you. Help me to release my preconceptions and fully immerse myself in the wisdom that awaits. Infuse my reading with your insight, opening my heart to the lessons that will foster my growth and deepen my joy. Grant me the big willingness I need to live out the teachings I am learning, to trust the process, and to make it fun — all the while reminding me not to make any struggle that I experience too real. Guide my understanding, highlight the passages that need my attention, and inspire the practical applications that will resonate most deeply. May this experience bring me closer to the boundless happiness I am destined to embrace.

Amen.

You Are Forgiving Deeper

"Forgiveness is the key to happiness. Here is the answer to your search for peace. Here is the key to meaning in a world that seems to make no sense. Here is the way to safety in apparent dangers that appear to threaten you at every turn and bring uncertainty to all your hopes of ever finding quietness and peace."
— ACIM Workbook for Students, Lesson 121

FORGIVENESS is undoubtedly our superpower in this cuckoo world, amigos, and the good news is that it's always just a non-judgmental thought away. Since publishing *Live Your Happy*, I've come to see just how essential forgiveness is in navigating the complexities of daily life, particularly in the roles that mean the most to me — as a wife and a mother.

Forgiving in the ACIM Way

Forgiveness as taught by *A Course in Miracles* goes beyond the traditional understanding of merely pardoning someone's actions. It is a profound spiritual practice that invites a shift in perception of the entire world as we see it, leading to inner peace and healing. The Course asserts that we chiefly need to forgive ourselves for believing we are separated from our inner divinity (God, that is). So forgiveness undoes our rock-bottom belief in separation, restoring awareness of our inherent unity and interconnectedness.

According to ACIM the world we perceive is an illusion — a projection of our own minds struggling to make sense of feeling abandoned. Our experiences are shaped by all our negative thoughts and beliefs of abandonment, and forgiveness is the tool to transform those perceptions. When someone behaves in a hurtful or unkind manner, it stems from their own fears and insecurities and is not a reflection of our true worth or identity.

Forgiveness is a choice we make to release our grievances, most of which stem from the ego's desire to protect itself and maintain a sense of separate identity. It is not about condoning or accepting harmful behavior, but about recognizing that our peace of mind is more valuable than holding onto anger, resentment, or judgment. In this regard, the Course gives us a handy tool for perceiving everything that other people may do: they are either expressing love, or issuing a call for love. It's up to us to remember that either way, love is the best and obvious answer. And when a call for love is very challenging to us, forgiveness is the best way to start.

Stepping into a Whirlwind

The year 2017 marked the beginning of a whirlwind chapter in my life. If you've read my first book, you know how much I longed for marriage and a child. Miraculously, it all happened. I met my husband Christian at a retreat; he not only supported my book launch but also became my partner. His help with getting the book out there brought us together. We were married and expecting our son, Ari, all within six months of meeting.

This rapid progression could have been overwhelming, yet forgiveness played a crucial role in navigating it all. For years, I sought someone to complete me because I didn't see myself as worthy. By the time Christian entered my life, my journey through forgiveness had equipped me with the tools to trust fully and love boldly.

Christian, who is German, can be strict and stern at times — yes, so much so that I jokingly say I want to throw him out the window! But instead, I practice the "F word" of forgiveness. It's not always easy — no way, José! Yet choosing forgiveness helps us step out of the cycle of suffering and conflict, even when it feels downright impossible.

There's so much more I could share about my relationship with Christian and the healing we've experienced. I'll save the juiciest bits for later, but know this: forgiveness is what transforms relationships and keeps real unconditional love alive.

Forgiveness in Daily Life

Forgiveness in daily life isn't a dramatic, one-time gesture with permanent results. It's a series of small, yet powerful choices that we make moment by moment. Here's a rundown of those choices.

Presence and Awareness: Forgiveness begins with the decision to become fully present. When you're truly in the moment, you're not dwelling on past hurts or fretting about the future. Forgiveness requires staying aware and catching yourself in conflicted moments before your thoughts spiral into resentment or hostility.

For example, there are times when I catch myself being a little short with my son, Ari. He's seven years old and full of curiosity, energy, and wonder. Sometimes when I'm preoccupied or stressed, I find myself reacting impatiently. In those moments, I pause and realize that I'm not being present — I'm just reacting from fear or frustration. I take a breath and remind myself that he's only seven, doing the best he can. I laugh at how I was unthinkingly expecting him to act like an adult. That simple shift in awareness allows me to soften, reconnect, and respond with love instead of judgment.

This practice of presence teaches me that forgiveness starts with self-awareness. When we catch ourselves in those unconscious moments and choose to be present, we not only free ourselves from guilt and frustration but also create space for love and understanding. It's a powerful way to diffuse conflict and foster connection — with ourselves and others.

Non-Judgment: One of the most powerful lessons I've learned is that practicing non-judgment is a proactive form of forgiveness. When we choose not to judge, we experience incredible freedom — suddenly, nothing's the matter! Practicing non-judgment allows us to walk through life seeing situations, people, and everything else clearly, without the cloud of our preconceptions.

For instance, a coaching client of mine, Ana, faced a situation where she felt betrayed by a friend who had shared a secret. Rather than stewing in anger and letting that betrayal define her friend entirely, Ana chose to step back from judging the situation. She considered her friend's actions within the context of her own fears and her fear of being judged. By refusing to judge her friend harshly and choosing to see the situation with love instead of fear, Ana found a profound sense of peace and forgiveness in place of her initial aggravation. This shift in perspective — seeing through a lens of non-judgmental understanding rather than condemnation — allowed her to genuinely forgive her friend, transforming a painful situation into a lesson in compassion and freedom.

Feeling Your Feelings: Embracing your emotions is a spiritual practice — and ignoring them, not so much. It's completely okay to feel hurt, angry, or upset. Forgiveness doesn't mean you have to ignore difficult feelings; it means you acknowledge them, feel them fully, and allow yourself the inner space to experience them without judgment. This approach is rooted in self-respect: recognizing and honoring your emotions as valid and important. Remember, as the saying goes, "this too shall pass." Feeling your feelings is a crucial step in the process of forgiveness because it's not about suppression; it's about liberation from those heavy emotions, allowing them to move through and out of you, leading to genuine healing and release.

The Practice of Letting Go and Trusting

Forgiveness fundamentally involves letting go. That means releasing our need for control and manipulation, and trusting a higher plan than we can come up with on our own. When we relinquish our urge to dictate outcomes and manipulate situations, we truly practice forgiveness. This is about trusting in God rather than assuming we know best, which liberates us from the heavy burden of a "God complex."

Accepting that the current moment is 'unfolding as it should' can bring a profound ease into our lives. Resistance to this acceptance only leads to struggle and frustration. Thus, the practice of letting God manage the universe while we simply trust and let go is vital. By releasing our hold on life's script, we find that everything necessary gets done, and what is meant to happen does... often far more beautifully than we could have orchestrated.

During times when the urge to control threatens to overwhelm me, or when negative emotions arise towards others, I find it helpful to engage in meditation or prayer. I sit quietly, close my eyes, and focus on trusting and releasing. I visualize sending love and light to the situation or person, repeating a mantra that reinforces my intention to trust in the divine unfolding: "I let go and trust that the highest good for me is unfolding now." This practice doesn't just alter my perception of things going wrong. It transforms my heart, allowing me to enjoy each moment and learn from the peace that true forgiveness brings.

Forgiveness Practice: Transforming Beliefs

This practice is inspired by Byron Katie, an author and teacher of transformative inquiry called The Work, which we will dive deeper into later. This will help guide you on a journey of release and peace.

Forgiveness doesn't just transform the situation; it transforms your heart. This practice is designed to help you identify and let go of the beliefs that disrupt your peace, creating space for clarity, love, and joy.

Before you begin, ensure that you have a journal and pen, and find a quiet space where you can focus without interruptions. Consider playing some relaxing music to create an environment for deep reflection.

1. **List Your Negative Beliefs:** Start by writing down all the negative beliefs that are currently disturbing your peace. Write these on the left side of your journal page.

2. **Write Opposing Loving Beliefs:** On the right side of the page, opposite each negative belief, write a positive, loving belief. For example, if one of your negative beliefs is *"I am not good enough,"* write *"I am good enough"* on the right side.

3. **Assess the Loving Beliefs:** For each pair of beliefs, reflect on how the loving thought might be truer than the negative thought. Write down reasons or situations where the positive belief has been or could be true. This helps to reinforce the validity and power of positive beliefs over the negative ones.

For example, a negative belief I struggled with was: *"I can't handle life."* To counter this, I affirmed the opposite: *"I can handle life."* As I reflected on this new, positive belief, I began to recognize all the evidence supporting it. I have successfully created and facilitated a powerful workshop, delivered an epic sermon at a Unity Church via Zoom, and developed a thriving membership platform for my community. I've managed my son

Ari's doctors' appointments and even kept up with everyday tasks like doing the dishes. The list goes on, clearly showing that the initial belief was just nonsense — seriously *caca*. This reflection helped me see that not only could I handle life, but I was already doing it quite effectively. This shift from a limiting belief to an empowering one is not just about feeling better; it's about recognizing and embracing the truth of our capabilities.

4. **Affirm and Release:** As you affirm new, positive beliefs, feel as if you are already living them fully. Write down and repeat statements like, "I choose to believe I am good enough because I have proven it in many ways." Close your eyes and see yourself as already being good enough. Imagine how that feels — how the confidence, peace, and strength of that belief settle into your body. You may even catch yourself smiling, as you recognize that you are stepping into your true reality of love. Visualize the negative emotions from the old beliefs dissolving, leaving your body and mind, as you fully embody the truth of who you are.

This practice is a powerful way to shift your mindset from self-criticism to self-acceptance and peace. By rewriting the narratives you hold about yourself, you engage in deep forgiveness — not just forgiving others, but forgiving yourself for having believed the negative thoughts that limited your happiness. Remember, when we forgive, we aren't just saying, *"It's okay."* We are declaring, *"I choose peace and happiness over holding onto pain."* This transformation is not only liberating but profoundly healing.

What Forgiveness Offers You

Embracing forgiveness offers us nothing less than true freedom. It reopens the door to the memory of God in our minds, reconnecting us with our divine essence. Through forgiveness, I have found the clarity and vision to transform what many might see as life's greatest pains into profound gifts. My father's suicide, once a source of deep sorrow, has become a lesson in resilience and compassion. My ectopic pregnancy, rather than a loss, revealed itself as a blessing, teaching me about the true nature of gain and loss. Even the end of my first marriage emerged as a grand opportunity for personal growth and learning, rather than a sign of failure.

These experiences, underpinned by the teachings of *A Course in Miracles*, have shown me that no matter how 'big' the ordeal, there is always a way to see it differently through the lens of forgiveness. This transformative perspective does not merely alter my view of life's events and

YOU ARE FORGIVING DEEPER

17

circumstances. It fundamentally changes my interactions with the world, allowing me to live with a lighter heart, free from the shackles of past grievances.

As we progress through this book, we'll explore various dimensions of forgiveness — from the personal to the collective, from forgiving others to ultimately forgiving ourselves. By understanding and applying the principles of ACIM, we can transform not only our relationships but our entire experience of life. Join me as we dive deeper into the transformative power of true forgiveness, where each moment free of judgment brings us closer to our happiest selves. Let's go!

You Are Questioning Every Thought

"I am never upset for the reason I think."
— ACIM Workbook for Students, Lesson 5

IF YOU'RE SEEING the quote above for the first time, you might find it offensive. But hold on — it's actually good news. We aren't really upset because of the unavoidable things happening to us or our around us; we're upset because of the stories we create about what's happening. This revelation is wonderful because it hands us the key to understanding the true cause of our suffering — and that's also the key to undoing that suffering.

So, the question is: Are you ready to stop playing the victim? Are you ready to take responsibility and live a happier life?

Yes? Great! Place your hand on your heart — your *corazón* — and say, *"I am willing and I am ready."*

Alright, let's dive in!

We can unravel the narratives that disrupt our peace

using a method that's as straightforward as it is profound — Byron Katie's Four Questions, or "The Work." This approach doesn't just complement the teachings of *A Course in Miracles*. The Work amplifies ACIM, providing a practical way to liberate ourselves from the chains of our misconceptions.

I'm all about learning and sharing anything that complements the Course, and as I mentioned earlier, The Work is like forgiveness on steroids! The fourth question, what she calls "the turnaround," provides an accelerated path to the forgiveness that ACIM teaches. That's why I'm so adamant about this and share The Work with my clients, my community, and now my readers.

How The Work Changed My Life

Years ago, even before I wrote *Live Your Happy*, I had heard of Byron Katie but never paid much attention to what she taught. Then one day, a quote of hers caught my eye on Facebook: "It's not the problem that causes our suffering; it's our thinking about the problem." That struck a chord with me, and I started to follow her work and picked up her book *Loving What Is*. At that time, I was going through a difficult period in my marriage with Christian. He was having doubts, and all my abandonment issues were surfacing full throttle. I even started to feel a depression creeping in, the likes of which I hadn't felt since my twenties. I thought, "No way," and dove headfirst into doing The Work.

As I worked on the thought *"I am scared Christian will leave me,"* applying the four questions not just once but repeatedly, I began to experience what *A Course in Miracles* describes as a miracle: a shift in perception from fear to love. It wasn't easy. I remember traveling, speaking at an event in Amsterdam, running retreats, and feeling unsettled in my marriage. Even while on a book tour in Mexico for *Vive Feliz*, the Spanish version of my book, I felt so insecure, and all the old feelings of insecurity were resurfacing.

During this time, doing The Work really helped me. It inspired me to write a letter to Christian that I couldn't send at first. Reading it now, I realize it was really addressed to myself...

Dear Christian,

I know things have been rocky between us, and I acknowledge that part of this is because of me, since I am responsible for my experience.

Your comments about me being lazy, unattractive, unmotivated, have hurt me deeply, making me defensive. Yet this serves as a gift. It reveals where the problem lies — in me.

I do believe I am lazy, unattractive, not good enough ... It's true. Very true that I believe this about myself. (It would be nice to have you hug me right here.)

So, I apologize for wanting you to be nice, gentle, to not say these things, to just love me for the way I am. I apologize for trying to impose things on you, for wanting you to change how you are with me.

I know you are doing the best you can. We all are.

My willingness is to stop the war with myself now. Hence, the war will stop with us. (I'm bringing up the white flag.)

Thank you for bringing ALL of these things to the surface for me. It's a true blessing in disguise.

I love you, and let me know how I can support you on your journey.

I'm in it to win the love within and the love that is US in God.

The time has come.

Love,

Maria

When people read this letter, they might wonder why Christian would say such things to me. Please understand he was sharing his feelings, not in a mean way, but as a cry for love. Looking back, I see that clearly. He was also feeling overwhelmed. He got married at 25, became a father at 26, and moved to Los Angeles from another country with no money or solid foundation. He was just expressing himself, and I took it personally. This is often how relationships end. We take things personally that aren't meant that way, and then never let go of the hurt.

This letter is a powerful demonstration of how I was internalizing his words — seeing them as a reflection of my own insecurities. If I didn't believe these negative things about myself, they wouldn't have bothered me. Everything that comes up, comes up for our healing. You hear me? And yes, it sucks big time... pero, let's start to look at it another way.

Introduction to The Work

The Work is a profound journey into the core of your thoughts. This simple yet powerful process of inquiry helps you identify and question the thoughts that cause your suffering. All you need is that BIG willingness, as I shared in my first book — just an open mind and a readiness to tackle those tough thoughts.

Practicing The Work is essentially practicing the F word: forgiveness. The four questions guide you straight to the part of your mind that is all about love, the part that's connected to God, your true nature, your innocence. It's like a direct line to rediscovering who you really are beneath all those *caca* thoughts!

Explanation of the Four Questions

Here are the four questions from The Work by Byron Katie, designed to challenge and transform your thinking:

1. *Is it true?* — Ask yourself if the thought you're thinking is actually true. This simple question begins the journey into questioning the reality of your perceptions.

2. *Can you absolutely know it's true?* — Challenge the certainty of your belief. This question starts to open the door to your sanity, urging you to look beyond superficial assumptions.

3. *How do you react — what happens — when you believe that thought?* — Observe the impact the belief has on your life and emotions. This step calls for deep honesty and vulnerability — no spiritual bypassing allowed! How do you treat others when you believe that thought? How do you treat yourself? Truly feel your feelings and recognize how they shape your reality.

4. *Who would you be without the thought?* — Imagine yourself in the absence of this stressful thought. Who would you be if you didn't even have the ability to think it? This powerful inquiry helps you see the possibility of a life unburdened by such beliefs and takes you to what *A Course in Miracles* describes as true forgiveness.

These questions invite deeper introspection and typically lead to a turnaround, which involves experiencing the opposite of what you originally believed.

The Turnaround

The turnaround is an essential part of The Work's inquiry process, conducted after the four questions have been thoroughly explored. This step involves taking the original thought and flipping it to its opposite (or several opposites) to uncover new perspectives and deeper truths. For instance, if your original thought was *"My partner doesn't listen to me,"* one turnaround could be *"I don't listen to my partner."* Another might be "I don't listen to myself." A third opposite: "My partner does listen to me." This reflection challenges you to consider your own role in the dynamics you experience, offering profound insights into how you contribute to your situations.

Engaging in the turnaround effectively can deepen the practice of forgiveness. It not only reveals areas of self-deception and misunderstanding but also highlights opportunities for personal growth and reconciliation with others. If approached with big willingness and openness, the turnaround takes you straight to heaven! *¡Si!*

How to Do The Work

To effectively do The Work, start with a specific situation that upsets you. You can write down your stressful thoughts about it on a Judge-Your-Neighbor Worksheet (downloadable at *https://tinyurl.com/yc4aw7nc*). Then, use the Four Questions above to begin the inquiry.

For instance, if you're upset because you have the thought *"My friend doesn't appreciate me,"* ask yourself each of the four questions regarding this thought. Allow each response to come from a deep, honest place.

Let's put this into practice now. Find a quiet place where you can sit undisturbed. Take a moment to write down a recent stressful situation. Also, write down your thoughts about it. Now apply each of the four questions to your thoughts:

1. *Is it true?*
2. *Can you absolutely know it's true?*
3. *How do you react when you believe this thought?*
4. *Who would you be without this thought?*

Reflect on each answer sincerely, and observe any new insights or feelings that arise. You might discover that your original thought isn't as true or as anchored in reality as you believed.

Now, try the turnaround: Take the original thought and flip it to explore its opposites. For example, if your thought was *"My partner doesn't respect me,"* you might turn it around to *"I don't respect my partner," "I don't respect myself,"* or *"My partner <u>does</u> respect me."* Explore these turnarounds and see if they might hold as much or more truth than your original thought. Reflect on how these new perspectives might change your reaction to the original situation.

YOU ARE QUESTIONING EVERY THOUGHT   **27**

This exercise not only challenges your initial perceptions but also opens up new avenues for healing and understanding. It's a powerful way to experience firsthand how the flexibility of your thoughts can lead to greater emotional freedom.

Doing The Work can be like setting off fireworks in your mind; it illuminates and clears away old patterns of thinking that no longer serve you. This simple yet profound practice has the power to transform your life, bringing more peace and less suffering. As you continue with these inquiries, you'll find a greater sense of freedom and clarity. Embrace this journey and let the understanding you gain light up your path in living your happiest! For more about The Work visit: *www.thework.com.*

Bridging The Work and ACIM's Forgiveness

You might be wondering how Byron Katie's four questions tie into the forgiveness teachings of the Course. Well, buckle up, mi gente, because we're about to connect the dots and reveal how these two powerful tools are like peanut butter and jelly — they just go together!

1. Is it true?

The Course encourages us to question the reality of our perceptions. It teaches that much of what we see and believe is filtered through the ego's lens of fear and separation. By asking, "Is it true?" we start to dismantle the illusions we've accepted as facts.

The very first Workbook lesson — "Nothing I see... means anything" invites us to recognize that our unexamined perceptions are not reliable.

2. Can you absolutely know it's true?

ACIM emphasizes that our ego's knowledge is limited and that only the Holy Spirit within us truly knows all. By admitting that we can't absolutely know the truth, we open ourselves to higher understanding. ACIM's Workbook lesson #25, "I do not know what anything is for" reminds us that our typically unreflective judgments are totally inadequate.

3. How do you react — what happens — when you believe that thought?

The Course teaches that our thoughts create our emotional experiences. When we believe fearful thoughts, we experience pain and separation. This question helps us see the cost of holding onto certain beliefs. ACIM Workbook lesson #5, *"I am never upset for the reason I think,"* highlights that our distress comes from our errant thoughts and not the external causes we'd like to blame.

4. Who would you be without the thought?

This is where the magic happens — true forgiveness enters the stage! ACIM defines forgiveness as letting go of the illusions and seeing with the eyes of love. By envisioning ourselves without a limiting thought, we step into a space of peace and unity. ACIM Workbook lesson #121, *"Forgiveness is the key to happiness"* reminds us that

You Are Questioning Every Thought   29

releasing our judgments restores the joy that is our spiritual birthright.

The Turnaround: A Path to Healing

After working through the questions, the turnaround is like the cherry on top. It flips our original thought, offering a new perspective and deeper self-awareness. This aligns with ACIM's emphasis on shifting perception from fear to love. At the beginning of the ACIM Text, miracle principle #42 states that *"A major contribution of miracles is their strength in releasing you from your false sense of isolation, deprivation and lack."* The turnaround facilitates this release, allowing us to experience a miracle in our thinking. *Pow!*

By integrating Byron Katie's four questions with the forgiveness teachings of *A Course in Miracles*, we create a powerful synergy that accelerates our healing journey. Both approaches guide us to question our thoughts, release judgments, and return to our natural state of love and peace. Understanding this connection is a game-changer. It means that every time you practice The Work, you're also embracing the essence of ACIM's forgiveness. You're not just scratching the surface — you're going deep-sea diving into the waters of true healing. And trust me, the treasures you find there are beyond worth it.

Sharing the Unsent Letter

So, remember that heartfelt letter I poured my soul into but didn't send to Christian right away? Well, it turns out that not sharing it immediately was a game-changer — for both of us.

At first, writing the letter was just a therapeutic act for me. It allowed me to process my emotions and take responsibility for my own feelings. By acknowledging that the hurtful things Christian said were mirroring my own insecurities, I began to heal from within. I was doing The Work on myself, and it was transforming me from the inside out.

After this process, I decided to share the letter with Christian. And let me tell you, that took some big courage! When I handed him the letter, I felt vulnerable but also hopeful. I wasn't sure how he'd react, but I knew that transparency was essential for our growth.

Christian read the letter thoughtfully. I could see a mix of emotions flicker across his face: surprise, empathy, maybe even a bit of guilt. When he finished, he looked at me with softened eyes and said, "I had no idea you felt this way."

We sat down and had one of the most honest conversations of our entire relationship. He shared his own fears and doubts — the pressure of marrying young, becoming a father, moving countries, and trying to find his footing without a solid foundation. He admitted that his

YOU ARE QUESTIONING EVERY THOUGHT   31

comments were more about his own insecurities than about me.

In that moment, we both realized that we had been projecting our fears onto each other. By sharing the letter, we opened a door to mutual understanding and compassion. It wasn't just healing for me; it was healing for us.

From that day forward, our relationship began to shift. We became more open with each other, expressing not just our frustrations but also our vulnerabilities. The defensive walls started to crumble, replaced by a stronger foundation built on trust and empathy.

I noticed that Christian became more mindful of his words, and I became less reactive. When disagreements arose, we approached them differently — more as a team tackling an issue rather than opponents in a battle.

By sharing the letter, I learned that being open and honest is a bridge to deeper connection. Keeping it to myself might have helped me heal individually, but sharing it allowed us to heal together. It turned out that he was craving the same openness but didn't know how to initiate it.

This experience reinforced the power of The Work and the teachings of *A Course in Miracles* for me. It showed me that when we take responsibility for our own perceptions and are uncompromising and share even though it's hard, we not only free ourselves but also give others the opportunity to do the same.

So, if you're hesitating to express your true feelings to someone important in your life, consider this a sign to go for it. The world needs your authenticity. Authenticity IS sexy! Remember, healing is a collective journey, and sometimes taking that first step can create ripples of transformation beyond what you ever imagined.

Well, now that you've mastered an epic way to practice the F word — forgiveness — it's time to dive deeper into what really keeps us from living our happiest lives. We've already explored quite a bit about why we suffer, and believe it or not, we're just on Chapter 2. But hold on tight inside the happy train because as we head to Chapter 3, you have to get ready for even more transformative insights. *Choo choo!* Let's chug deeper into understanding and healing as we continue this journey toward living our happiest life!

You Are Free from Judgment

*"Judgment and love are opposites. From one come
all the sorrows of the world. But from the other
comes the peace of God Himself."*
— from ACIM Workbook Lesson 352

LEARNING NON-JUDGMENT has been a game-changer in my life. When we let go of judgment, we live our happiest lives — truly! Judgment keeps us stuck in a cycle of suffering, and letting it go is key to finding peace. But here's the deal: to stop judging, we need to be vigilant and have BIG willingness.

In this chapter, we're going to dive deep into the practice of non-judgment — what it looks like, how it changes your life, and how you can bring it into your everyday moments.

Being judgmental can feel like our natural state, right? That's the tricky part. It's like our default setting, always triggering us to react and draw conclusions. But here's the truth we need to meet: judgment is not our natural state. Love is. Judgment only came into play with the invention of the ego, and somewhere along the line, we started believing that we need judgment to protect ourselves. There is another way, and that way is choosing love instead.

But in order to do that, we need to get really good at catching ourselves in the act. This is where *vigilance*, as the Course defines it, becomes essential. We have to be on guard, not in a stressful way, but with awareness and a sense of presence. This kind of vigilance helps us stay alert to our ego's tendency to judge. The more we practice that self-observant presence, the more likely we are to catch ourselves before the judgment slips out.

Let's dive into why vigilance is the key to letting go of judgment — and how it has the power to transform our daily lives.

Learning Vigilance

In *A Course in Miracles*, vigilance means keeping a constant and caring watch over our thoughts. It's about being alert to the mind's tendency to drift toward fear, judgment, and other ego-based reactions, and then consciously choosing love and peace instead. The Course reminds us that the mind is incredibly powerful; wherever we focus our attention is where we create our reality. This is why it instructs, "Be vigilant only for God and His Kingdom." That means we have to keep our mind focused

YOU ARE FREE FROM JUDGMENT

35

on love, truth, and forgiveness.

But let's be real — this isn't always easy. It can feel like we're constantly playing whack-a-mole with our judgmental thoughts! One minute you're feeling all Zen, and the next, you're judging the person in front of you for walking too slow at the grocery store. It happens to the best of us!

Learning vigilance doesn't mean we'll never judge again. What it means is that we learn to notice when judgment sneaks in, so we can choose differently. We get to practice catching ourselves before judgment takes over. And trust me, the more we practice, the better we get at this.

Let's say you're driving (always a good time for judgment to take the wheel, right?) and someone cuts you off. Instantly, your first thought might be, "What a jerk!" That's the judgment of your ego trying to protect itself while also looking for a reason to justify its frustration, and feel superior too.

But with vigilance, you can catch that thought before it spirals out of control. You can pause, breathe, and ask yourself, "What if this has nothing to do with me? What if they're in a hurry for a good reason?" You might even go so far as to bless them in your mind, sending them love instead of anger. That's what vigilance for love looks like. You shift from ego to spirit in a heartbeat, and that, my friends, is where the happy happens!

Tips for Practicing Vigilance

1. **Catch yourself quickly.** The first step in practicing vigilance is awareness. You can start your day by setting an intention to notice any judgmental thoughts as soon as they arise. The quicker you catch them, the less likely they are to take over.
2. **Pause and breathe.** When you've noticed a judgment arising, pause and take a breath. This helps break the automatic reaction and gives you a chance to respond differently.
3. **Ask for help.** You're not in this alone. Ask the Holy Spirit (or whatever you call your inner guide) to help you see the situation differently. Remind yourself of the ACIM principle "I am determined to see things differently." Let this be your mantra when judgment shows up.
4. **Turn it into love.** Once you've caught a judgment and paused to breathe, choose to send love instead. In most cases this will be a simple, silent choice — but this small act can change the energy of a situation in a big way. Love transforms everything.

YOU ARE FREE FROM JUDGMENT   37

Being vigilant takes practice, but the more we do it, the more natural it becomes. It's like working out a muscle. At first it feels like you're lifting the weight of the world. But soon enough, that muscle gets stronger, and you'll notice yourself catching judgments faster. Each time you choose love over judgment, you're reprogramming your mind to align more with your true nature. And that's where real freedom is — living from love, not judgment.

Big Willingness

In my first book I introduced the concept of Big Willingness as the first step to connect with the Holy Spirit. But here's the thing: Big Willingness isn't just for connecting with Spirit — it's a super-power you can use in every area of your life. Whether it's letting go of judgment, making a big life decision, or healing a relationship, willingness is the key that unlocks real transformation.

A Course in Miracles says that all you need is a little willingness to see miracles happen. I like to kick that up a notch and say "big, fat willingness"— because in this cuckoo world, we need a heavyweight willingness to create real change. You can apply it anywhere, to anything that has value for your growth.

Willingness is the engine that gets you where you want to go. You don't need to know how everything will change; you just need to be willing. When you're willing, you're telling the Universe that you're open to seeing things differently, and that's where the miracles begin. Whether it's letting go of judgment, forgiving someone, or taking a big leap in life, it all starts with being willing.

A Prayer for Big Willingness

Let's bring this practice into focus with a short prayer you can use whenever you feel resistance to letting go of judgment:

Dear Holy Spirit,

I come to you with a big willingness to see things another way. I am ready to let go of my judgments, even the ones I really want to hold onto. Help me see this situation through the eyes of love, and guide me to choose peace instead of fear. I trust that with my willingness, miracles are already happening.

Thank you, Amen.

Once you declare that you're willing to change, even just a little, you've already put yourself on the path to transformation. Keep showing up with big willingness, and watch how everything starts to shift.

Willingness in the Course

In *A Course in Miracles*, willingness is a recurring theme — it's the golden key that unlocks the door to divine guidance. The Course teaches us that we don't need to do everything on our own (*Gracias Dios mio!*), but we

YOU ARE FREE FROM JUDGMENT   **39**

do need to be willing to listen. In ACIM, the Holy Spirit is described as the Voice for God, a divine presence that bridges the gap between our perceived separation from God and the truth of our oneness with Him. The Holy Spirit is not seen as a separate being but rather as the communication link between our mind and God, constantly guiding us back to love, truth, and peace.

With willingness, we open ourselves to receive guidance from the Holy Spirit. This guidance is what takes us from judgment to non-judgment, from fear to love.

When we practice big willingness, we're saying to the Holy Spirit, *"I'm ready to be led. Show me another way."* And here's the beautiful part: the Course teaches that when we ask for guidance, we'll always be shown a way that leads us to peace. But it all starts with that willingness to listen, and trust in what we are told.

The ego, on the other hand, loves to keep us in judgment of everyone and everything, including ourselves. It's how that fearful part of our mind stays alive. But with big willingness, we hand that habit of fearfulness over to the Holy Spirit and say, "I'm willing to see this differently." When we open up to guidance, we allow ourselves to be led out of judgment and into clarity. That's where true non-judgment lives — not in trying to figure everything out on our own, but in being willing to follow the guidance we're given.

Being a Course student is not about how much we

know or how "spiritual" we can be. It's about how willing we are to let go of control and allow guidance to take over. The Course often says, "You need do nothing." That doesn't mean we sit back and let life just happen to us. It means we release the need to control outcomes and instead be willing to listen. The more willing we are to listen, the easier it is to live without judgment. We begin to see that judgment was never really natural — it was just the ego trying to maintain its grip on us.

By choosing willingness over judgment, we are choosing to trust that the guidance we receive will always lead us back to peace. This is how we practice non-judgment: not by forcing ourselves to think differently, but by being willing to be shown another way. When we do this, miracles happen. Judgment fades away, and we return to our natural state of love.

Releasing Judgment of Yourself

"God is but love, and therefore so am I."
— ACIM Workbook Review V

One of the most profound teachings of the Course is that we *are* love, plain and simple. The Course is constantly reminding us that our true nature is love, light, and perfection. But here's the hard truth: most of the time we don't believe it. We've been trained by the ego to see ourselves as

YOU ARE FREE FROM JUDGMENT 41

flawed, broken, and not good enough. We are often vicious with ourselves, listening to an internal narrative that's anything but loving. We judge our bodies, our abilities, our worth. And all that is *no bueno*.

When we judge ourselves, we close off the flow of love. We tend to think that being hard on ourselves will make us do better, but it only keeps us stuck in suffering, where we can do very little. Becoming free of judgment begins with recognizing that you are love — always have been, always will be. The judgments you have of yourself are just old ego stories trying to keep you small.

So, how do we stop judging ourselves and come back to love? Here's a simple process:

1. **Catch the Judgment:** Using your well-developed vigilance, notice when you're being hard on yourself. Maybe you didn't meet a deadline, maybe you made a mistake, or maybe you're just not feeling "good enough" today. Whatever it is, catch it. Awareness is key.

2. **Acknowledge the Fear:** Every judgment begins with fear. Ask yourself, "What am I afraid of right now? Am I afraid I'm not lovable? Not capable?" Bringing the fear into the light helps to dissolve it.

3. **Forgive Yourself:** Forgiveness is the bridge that takes us from judgment to love. ACIM

teaches us that forgiveness is key to releasing all grievances — including the ones we hold against ourselves. When you forgive yourself, you're saying, "I am worthy of love, exactly as I am."

4. **Choose Love Instead:** This is where your Big Willingness comes in. You have to want to let go of the judgment and choose love instead. It's not always easy, but with practice, it gets easier. Say to yourself, "I choose to see myself through the eyes of love."

Releasing Judgment of Others

Once we start to release judgment of ourselves, it naturally becomes easier to stop judging others. Here's the kicker though: judging others is often a reflection of the judgments we hold against ourselves. That's why when we're critical of someone else, it's worth pausing to ask, "What does this say about how I feel about myself?"

The Course teaches us that when we judge others, we are seeing them through the eyes of the ego, not through the eyes of love. The ego is just part of our mind, a part that serves only fear; and it's really not the biggest part, even when it seems to be. Every judgment of another person is really a projection of our own fears and insecurities, another attempt by the ego to keep control of our mind. This is why it's so important to first work on how we see ourselves — because the more love we hold for ourselves, the more love we have for others.

Here's how we can work on letting go of judgment towards others:

1. **Catch Yourself in the Act:** Just like with self-judgment, awareness is key. Notice when you're judging someone. Maybe you're rolling your eyes at a slow driver (again??) or getting annoyed with a friend who said something weird. Whatever it is, catch it.

2. **Pause and Breathe:** This may sound familiar: Before you react, pause. Take a deep breath. This simple action creates space between the judgment and your response, giving you a chance to choose differently.

3. **Ask for Guidance:** Ask the Holy Spirit to help you see this person differently. Remember the lesson: *"I am determined to see things differently."* Use this as your prayer. Be willing to see the person through the eyes of love, not judgment.

4. **Remember That We're All Doing Our Best:** Most of the time, people are just doing the best they can with what they know. Before you judge someone, try to put yourself in their shoes.

Maybe they're having a tough day, maybe they're maybe they're carrying burdens you can't see. Compassion goes a long way toward softening our judgments.

5. **Send Them Love:** Instead of judgment, choose love. Silently send love to the person you were just judging. It might feel awkward at first, but it works. This simple practice can transform your relationships and your perspective.

By releasing judgment — of ourselves first, and then of others — we free ourselves from the heavy burden of the ego. The more we choose love over judgment, the more peace we experience in our daily lives. And when we catch ourselves slipping into judgment, we always have the opportunity to pause, breathe, and choose again.

Forgiveness Is That Easy!

I can't believe I'm sharing this already in Chapter 3, but I know you're ready for it and can totally handle it. Here's the thing: I struggled with forgiveness for years — seriously, years and years! I would read the Course lessons, apply them, do the work, but something always felt a little hard to grasp. I kept thinking, "How do I actually do this forgiveness thing?" It wasn't until I really dove deep into studying, applying, and living the teachings that I realized something that changed everything for me.

You know what forgiveness is, in very simple terms? I mean, seriously, it couldn't be easier...

NON-JUDGMENT. That's it. Non-judgment is the forgiveness that the Course is teaching. *¡Comprende?*

It's as simple as that. When we stop judging, we're forgiving. It's not some complex spiritual equation — it's just about letting go of the judgments we place on ourselves, on others, and on the world. When we choose to release judgment, we're choosing forgiveness.

The Course teaches that forgiveness is the key to inner peace, and it's not about forgiving everyone's unpleasant actions in the way we might think. Instead, it's about letting go of the belief in separation, that is, the idea that we're disconnected from each other or from love. Forgiveness, as ACIM defines it, isn't about pardoning someone for what they did or excusing bad behavior. It's about recognizing that everything we perceive as hurtful comes from the illusion of separation. The only thing we truly need to forgive is this illusion.

Here's the connection: every time we judge ourselves or others, we're reinforcing that illusion of separation. We're saying, "You and I are not the same," or "I am not worthy of love." But when we choose non-judgment, we see through that illusion. We start to perceive ourselves and others as part of the same love, the same wholeness.

When we let go of judgment, we are letting go of the grievances and stories that keep us stuck in fear. Non-judgment brings us back to our natural state of love. This is why the Course says, "Forgiveness is the key to happiness." True forgiveness, then, is simply the act of releasing judgment. It's not complicated or heavy; it's about choosing to see through the eyes of love instead of fear.

So, next time you catch yourself in judgment — whether it's toward yourself or someone else — remember this: letting go of judgment is the act of forgiveness. You don't need to do anything else. Just stop judging, and that's forgiveness in its purest, pro-active form.

So there you have it! Non-judgment and forgiveness are one and the same. The more we release judgment, the more we embrace the peace and happiness that are our natural state. As I mentioned, it took me years to figure this out, but now you have a simple way to understand ACIM forgiveness — so you can skip the long learning curve and dive straight into practicing it. You're welcome!

You Are Embracing All of You

Your task is not to seek for love, but merely to seek and find all of the barriers within yourself that you have built against it. – ACIM T-16.IV.6

As we dive into the idea of embracing all parts of ourselves — our perceived flaws, strengths, and everything in between — it's essential to realize that the struggle often lies in our resistance to what is. True acceptance isn't about forcing ourselves to love every part of life, but about recognizing the barriers we've built that keep us from seeing things as they truly are. The Course is teaching us to let go of all the barriers to love — because only love is real. This is our only job, our only purpose: to remember this truth.

I love that Byron Katie says, "The way you look blesses the world." Why? Because the way you are, just as you are, is a blessing. The way you look, the way you move through life, your unique essence — all this is your gift to the world. It's not something to fix or change; it's something to honor. When we stop trying to control or mold ourselves into what we think we should be, we open up to the truth that we are already whole, already enough. As the Course puts it in Workbook Lesson #187, *"I bless the world because I bless myself."*

The suffering we experience doesn't come from what happens to us but from our reactions and resistance to it. It's the stories we tell ourselves, the judgments we make, and the expectations we hold onto that create inner turmoil. When we learn to release these stories and stop trying to control everything, we open the door to deeper peace and happiness.

This chapter is about stepping into a space of surrender, where we stop fighting reality and start embracing life as it comes. This embrace begins at home: letting go of the need to fix or change yourself, and instead meeting yourself with love and acceptance right where you are. It's only when we accept our whole selves, flaws and all, that we can begin to experience true freedom and joy.

Here's the good news: If you are reading this book, you are ready to accept yourself. You are ready to release anything and everything that takes you away from love and makes you fall asleep to your only true reality. As you read this, remember: your willingness is everything. If deep in your heart, you truly want to love yourself as God, as the Divine loves you, then just pause for one second right here. Put your hand on your heart and say:

I am ready. I am ready to experience all of myself, my true self. I am ready to love my face, my nose, my big belly, my crooked nose, and my big butt fully and completely. I don't want to be or look like anyone else. I want this reality, as this IS what I have chosen. So, I stop the BS NOW and jump onto the embracing-all-of-me train... the other way just hurts too much. No more — I want to honor and love myself now!

Why We Don't Embrace Ourselves

At the core of the struggle to accept ourselves lies a simple yet profound truth: we have forgotten who we really are. *A Course in Miracles* teaches that the world began when the Son of God "forgot to laugh" at the strange world that seems so real. In that moment of forgetting, we slipped into a belief in separation: that we are somehow broken, flawed, and disconnected from love. This is the root of all our suffering. We've fallen into the illusion of being separate from love, from God, and from our true nature. From that misperception arises the entire world that we experience daily.

Conditioned by society, past experiences, and our own fears, we've been led to believe that we're not enough. We judge ourselves, believing that we need to be something other than what we are. It's this constant comparison, this endless measuring of ourselves against impossible standards, that makes us feel inadequate, unworthy, and unlovable.

But all of this stems from one simple mistake: we forgot to laugh. We forgot that none of this is real — none of our judgments or illusions define us — and in that forgetting, we lost sight of our divine essence.

All judgment stems from the belief that we are separate from love, from others, and from our true selves. Judgment is the habitual preoccupation of the ego, which thrives on the illusion of separation. It feeds on fear and scarcity, convincing us that we must constantly strive to be better, more perfect, more acceptable. But these are illusory goals created not to lead us forward in life, but to keep us stuck in a cycle of suffering. That's why we seem plagued by an endless variety of problems:

"No one could solve all the problems the world appears to hold. They seem to be on so many levels, in such varying forms and with such varied content, that they confront you with an impossible situation. Dismay and depression are inevitable as you regard them. Some spring up unexpectedly, just as you think you have resolved the previous ones. Others remain unsolved under a cloud of denial, and rise to haunt you from time to time, only to be hidden again but still unsolved." — ACIM W-79.5:1-5

All these problems begin with hating ourselves because we believe we are lacking, that we are inherently messed up, and that we need to fix or change who we are

YOU ARE EMBRACING ALL OF YOU **51**

to be loved. And that makes the whole world seem like an impossible problem. But this belief is the barrier to love itself. The truth is that we are already whole, already complete, already love. It's the stories we tell ourselves about not being good enough, not being attractive enough, not being successful enough that keep us trapped in self-hate.

The ego wants us to believe that our worth is tied to something external — our appearance, our achievements, our status. But *A Course in Miracles* tells us that our worth is inherent. It is given by God, by the Divine, and it can never be taken away. The challenge is to remember this truth in a world that constantly tells us otherwise.

Meet the Insecure Supermodel

When I was sixteen I started modeling. By the world's standards, I had what might be called the "perfect" face and body. I was tall, long-legged, and weighed 125 pounds (I have never seen that weight again! LOL). But here's the kicker: even though I looked like the so-called ideal, I was plagued by insecurity.

I remember one moment like it was yesterday. I was chosen from 10,000 girls as one of the top ten finalists in a contest for YM (Young & Modern) magazine. There I was in New York City, standing amongst the best of the best. But guess what? I was absolutely riddled with uncertainty and fear. You know how people say a picture is worth a thousand words? Well, you can literally see my insecurity in the magazine — I didn't even smile in the photo! Imagine that: I was chosen from thousands of girls, and yet I was too insecure to smile.

This story is the perfect illustration of the fact that what we look like has nothing to do with our real truth, with who we are. Our insecurity doesn't come from how we look; it comes from what we're thinking and believing about ourselves. I didn't feel beautiful even if I fit the world's definition of beauty. And why? Because the insecurity was coming from the thoughts I was holding onto: "I'm not good enough," "I'm not pretty enough," and "I don't belong here." As the Course instructs, *"It is with your thoughts, then, that we must work, if your perception of the world is to be changed."* (ACIM W-23.1:5)

Now, over thirty years later, with 45 more pounds and some wrinkles on my face, I feel more beautiful than ever. And it has nothing to do with how I look, but everything to do with what I am thinking and believing about myself.

Pero, I'm not perfect at this yet! There are still moments when I get insecure about my body and looks, especially with my husband being fifteen years younger. I catch myself thinking, "Maybe he'd prefer to be with a thin, blonde girl his age." When that happens, my job is to turn inward and do self-inquiry: Is it true? Well, it sure doesn't look like it — he's married to me, after all. LOL! These moments are opportunities for me to practice letting go of judgment, remembering that what I believe about myself creates my experience.

Our confidence comes from our minds, not our bodies. Our bodies and looks are just statues and images, nothing more. If they really mattered, then why do famous actors commit suicide? Why do models become alcoholics or go under the knife for plastic surgery they don't even need? How we look can never give us real confidence or happiness. It's our connection to love, to God, that does.

That doesn't mean we don't need to take care of our bodies. Of course we do! We feed them the best foods, we exercise — that's what love does. But we don't let our bodies define us. We don't make the mistake of thinking that how we look determines our worth. Because, come on: we are so much more than that!

Exercise:
Head Dump & Handing It Over to Spirit

In my first book, we did an exercise called "Big Deals." Now we're going to do something similar but take it even deeper. This time, we're tackling the thoughts that are weighing us down. This is the stuff we don't want to admit out loud because it feels too ugly or too real. So, here's your task: I want you to do a head dump and put ALL your flaws and insecurities on paper. Everything! (And no spiritual bypassing here. Be brutally honest.)

Thoughts you might have: *I am fat. I am unattractive. I am unhealthy. I am alone. I am unlovable.*

Now throw all that up, then onto the page!

Why? Because the time has come to get real. All these thoughts are making you sick. They are poisoning your mind, your body, and your connection to love. So dump them out. Let them spill onto the paper because this is the first step to healing.

Once you've written everything down, here's what follows: silence. Go into the silence where you can access the guidance of your Inner Teacher, the Holy Spirit. This voice is the answer to the ego's nauseating judgments. The Course tells us that the Holy Spirit's role is to bring us back to our right mind, to the truth of who we are. So now you ask the Holy Spirit: What is really true? And just listen. Let the Spirit show you how incredible, beautiful, powerful, and unlimited you are. Let Spirit remind you that you are the light of the world!

Here's my example:

Caca Thoughts
- *I don't like my belly.*
- *My hair isn't long or thick enough anymore.*
- *I have to cover my grays every single month!*
- *I feel fat and unattractive.*

> *Holy Spirit's Answer*
> - *Darling, you are beautiful. No, wait — no more beautiful could you be!*
> - *You are love. You are God's creation.*
> - *Your tummy, your hair, your everything is as perfect as it's meant to be. You are not your body — you are the light!*
>
> Feel the shift? This is what happens when we stop letting our ego tell us who we are and start letting Spirit do the talking. Let go of the caca and embrace the truth.

Letting Go of the Need to Be 'Perfect'

One of the most common barriers to self-acceptance is our relentless need to control. We want to control how we look, how others perceive us, and how life unfolds. At the root of this is the belief that if we can just get everything to fall perfectly into place, then we will finally be happy. But this quest for perfection is exhausting, and it keeps us from the very thing we seek: peace.

A Course in Miracles reminds us that the need for control is a defense mechanism of the ego. The ego tells us that if we can control every detail of our existence, then we can protect ourselves from hurt, disappointment, and rejection. But in reality, this need for control stems from the fear-driven beliefs that we aren't good enough as we are, that life won't give us what we want, that love will be withheld unless we're perfect.

I've been there. So many times in my life, I've tried to control how people see me. I've agonized over my body, my appearance, and the way I present myself, believing that if I could just get everything 'right,' then maybe I'd be enough. But that's not how life works. No matter how hard I tried to be perfect on the outside, I still felt like something was missing. Because the truth is that the happiness and peace I was seeking would never come from controlling my external world.

When we let go of the need to control, we give ourselves permission to be exactly as we are. This doesn't mean we stop taking care of ourselves or working toward goals, but we release the illusion that our worth depends on achieving perfection. Instead, we begin to trust that we are enough just as we are, and that life is unfolding exactly as it needs to.

As Byron Katie says, "When you argue with reality, you lose — but only 100% of the time." This has been such a powerful reminder for me. All those years of trying to control my looks, my relationships, my circumstances amounted to arguing with reality. I was trying to mold the world to fit my idea of how things 'should' be. But the more I've learned to let go and trust the flow of life, the more peace I have experienced.

Control is a form of resistance, and resistance always

leads to suffering. When we resist life as it is, and resist ourselves as we are, we're basically telling the universe that we don't trust it. We're saying that we believe we know better than God or the Divine what should happen. You have to understand that everything is unfolding for your highest good, whether you can see it or not. When we embrace this idea, we begin to loosen our grip on control and open ourselves to the flow of love and grace.

Letting go of control also frees us from the constant self-criticism that comes from striving for perfection. Perfection is an illusion, and chasing it only leads to disappointment and frustration. Instead, we can choose to embrace our imperfections, knowing that they are part of what makes us human. As we release the need to be 'perfect,' we discover the beauty of being authentic.

Our authenticity, our willingness to show up as we are, flaws and all, is what makes us truly beautiful. It's in our vulnerability, not our perfection, that we connect most deeply with ourselves and others.

The Epic Ending: You Are Already Perfect

Here's the truth bomb: You are already perfect. Yes, YOU — just as you are, right now. *A Course in Miracles* tells us: "*Nothing real can be threatened. Nothing unreal exists.*" What does that mean? It means that your true beauty, your worth, your divine perfection can never be threatened by a big belly, gray hair, or the number on a scale. That's all just ego fluff: forms of unreality.

The real you — the you that's connected to God — cannot be touched by any of that. So, the more you remember this, the more you wake up to who you truly are. And here's the truth amigo: the more you start to believe it, the more your life will reflect it.

Now, as you go forward, when those sneaky little judgments pop up (because let's be real, they will), just don't get stuck in them. Pause. Breathe. And ask yourself: *What would Spirit say about me right now?* Then listen, because Spirit will always tell you the truth: You are love. You are whole. You are already complete.

The caca thoughts? Let them pass like dirty clouds. They aren't real. What's real is the light inside of you, the love that you are, and the limitless potential you hold.

So, let's go all in. No more holding back. Embrace all of you: the messy parts, the beautiful parts, the parts you're still learning to love. Because, baby, this is it. This is where true freedom begins. And guess what? You are so, so worthy of it.

¡Vamonos!

You Are Healing Your Relationships

"When you meet anyone, remember it is a holy encounter. As you see him, you will see yourself. As you treat him, you will treat yourself. As you think of him, you will think of yourself. Never forget this, for in him you will find yourself or lose yourself." — ACIM, T-8.III.4

THE WORLD is a classroom, and relationships are the master class. Or, to put it another way: No one can trigger us or push our buttons quite like those closest to us, right? The happy news is: those buttons are actually golden opportunities for healing. Our relationships — be they with our partners, family, friends, or even that annoying neighbor — hold the key to waking up, to remembering who we truly are.

ACIM teaches us that every encounter is a chance for healing. It's in the moments when we're tempted to point the finger and say, "It's your fault" that we are actually being invited to look within and see where we're blocking love. The Course suggests, "You are never upset for the reason you think." That is, our upset is not about what another person did or didn't do; it's about how we're choosing to see the situation. Relationships give us everything we need to heal everything.

So, are you ready to stop trying to be right in relationships? Are you willing to see that maybe, just maybe, the problem isn't your partner, or your mother-in-law, or your ex? Are you ready to step out of victim mode and into a space where you can truly experience love, peace, and yes, even happiness, in your relationships?

Bueno, dale que se puede! Let's do this. Let's dive in and explore how to shift our perspective in relationships, embrace forgiveness, and live our happiest in relationships.

Special Relationships: The Ego's Playground

The Course is not shy about calling out the ego's tricks, and one of its favorite playgrounds is the "special" relationship. These are the relationships where we place our happiness in someone else's hands — the "I need you to complete me" kind of relationships. If you're anything like me, you've had a few of these!

A special relationship can show up as that romantic partner who's going to fix all your problems, or that friend whose approval you need to feel worthy. The Course says, "The special relationship is the ego's most boasted gift."

YOU ARE HEALING YOUR RELATIONSHIPS **61**

Why? Because it's based on lack, need, and dependency. When we start trying to make someone else our source of happiness, confidence or safety, we're setting ourselves up for pain.

Special relationships create a rollercoaster effect: one minute you're on cloud nine, the next you're spiraling into despair because that person didn't call you back or didn't live up to your expectations. The problem with special relationships is that they keep us focused on the outside, instead of looking at what really needs healing within. They keep us stuck in the illusion that we're incomplete.

Martha's Story: From Seeking to Self-Love

My client Martha came to me feeling mucho lost in her relationship. She'd been dating a guy who she believed was her ticket to happiness, and thought that if they just got married, she'd finally feel complete. But every time he was distant or didn't respond to her texts right away, she'd be thrown into a panic. She'd obsess over every word he said, wondering if he was pulling away, because she wasn't enough.

Martha was stuck in a special relationship. Her happiness depended on his attention, his approval, and his love. And let me tell you, that is one exhausting way to live. As we worked together, I asked her to look at her feelings honestly — was it really all about him, or was it about the fear and unworthiness she carried within herself?

In one session, I had Martha write down the thought that was causing her the most pain: "He is everything, and without him, I am nothing." We took that thought into inquiry, and I asked her the first question of Byron Katie's Work, "Is it true?" Of course, in the moment, her answer was a resounding "Yes!" But then I asked her to take it deeper: "Can you absolutely know it's true?"

This is where the shift began. As she sat with the question, she started to see how it might not be entirely true. She remembered some earlier times, before he came into her life, when she had felt content and joyful. She thought of moments when she felt proud of her achievements, when she had friends and family who made her feel loved and seen. And then she realized that those feelings didn't come from him. They came from within her.

Martha began to realize that this thought — that he was the source of her happiness — was just an ego trick. The ego loves to convince us that our happiness lies outside of us, but *A Course in Miracles* teaches that happiness is our natural state, waiting to be uncovered. We don't need anyone else to give it to us. When Martha could see this, she began to loosen her grip on her attachment to him. She saw that she didn't need him to validate her worth. Instead, she could choose to validate herself.

I asked her to close her eyes, put her hand on her heart, and give over this thought to the Holy Spirit: "Holy Spirit, show me another way to see this. Help me to remember that I am already complete." She took a deep breath, and as she released the thought, she felt a weight lift from her chest. It wasn't a magical, instant cure — but it was the beginning of a shift toward reclaiming her power.

As Martha continued to work with this practice, she began to see the relationship differently. She stopped needing him to be her source of happiness and started seeing him as a companion on her journey — a fellow traveler, not her savior. And this shift of perception changed everything. She stopped panicking when he didn't text back immediately. She began to spend time doing things she loved on her own, rediscovering her passions and her sense of self-worth. Most importantly, she began to treat herself with the same love and attention she had been so desperately seeking from him.

This is the work, my friends. It's not about just knowing that you're whole; it's about experiencing it. It's about questioning those painful thoughts, giving them over to Spirit, and letting the truth emerge in their place. When Martha realized that she could be happy regardless of his actions, she broke free from the chains of her special relationship and began to cultivate a deeper, more genuine love for herself.

That's when the real magic happened. The relationship improved — not because he changed, but because she did. She no longer needed him to fill a void, and that took the pressure off him. She became lighter, more open, more present. From there they were able to build a connection that wasn't based on neediness, but on genuine love and respect.

What is Love for REAL?

Growing up, I thought love was everything the romance movies fed to us. One of my favorite film scenes was from "Jerry Maguire," when Tom Cruise says to Renée Zellweger, "*You complete me.*" I would melt during that part. For a long time, I believed that love was sacrifice. I thought love meant: *You behave the way I want you to behave*, or: *Show me you love me by doing this or that.* I could go on and on.

Relationships have always fascinated me, probably because they've been my biggest challenge. I spent years in a fruitless search for validation, approval, and the need to be recognized and loved — and even worse trying to convince others to love me. I explored this a lot in my first book with the 'Abs Guy' story. The world teaches us that love looks like approval, like validation through actions, but what I've come to realize on my journey is that love is freedom.

Real love lets people be as they are. It doesn't impose conditions or expectations. It allows the other person to be where they are in their journey. In my relationship with Christian, I often say a prayer: "Spirit, show me what real love is." This is my goal — not the Hollywood love I grew up with, but real, divine love.

Real love, as I've learned, is about healing together. It's about letting Christian push all my buttons so I can wake up to the truth of who I am. I want to love him without conditions, without the need to make him 'mine' or have him act a certain way. If we're together, great, if we're not, great. This is love. Real love. The kind that I'm ready and willing to embrace.

Love's Real Playground: Holy Relationships

The Course introduces the concept of the "holy relationship," and this is where the magic happens. A holy relationship happens when we shift our perspective by inviting the Holy Spirit into our connection with another person. It's when we stop using a special relationship to get something and start seeing it as an opportunity to give love, and to see with eyes of compassion.

A holy relationship is about recognizing that the love you want is already within you. Meaning: joining with another person from a place of wholeness, rather than neediness. ACIM says, "A holy relationship is a major step toward the perception of the real world." We take that step when we allow a relationship to become a mirror that shows us where we still have healing work to do. At that point, we choose to see through the eyes of love instead of judgment.

This doesn't mean that a holy relationship is all

rainbows and butterflies. Nope! It can actually be super challenging, because it requires us to look at our insecurities, our fears, all the walls we've built around our hearts. But here's the good news: in a holy relationship, we get to do this work together. We get to see each other's wounds and still choose love. It's the ultimate spiritual journey with a partner.

My Story with Christian

Let me share a story from my own life that shows what a holy relationship looks like in real time. One day, I was in the kitchen working on an upcoming retreat when Christian and I started discussing something... honestly, I don't remember what it was. But I do remember how the conversation shifted, and suddenly he responded to me in a mean way. I felt hurt, and my defenses immediately kicked in. My heart started racing and my mind filled with thoughts like: *He shouldn't be speaking to me like that.*

When Christian left the room, I made the effort to observe myself reacting. I noticed the pain and the defensiveness bubbling up inside. I witnessed my old abandonment issues rear their ugly head, but instead of drowning in those feelings, I let myself ride them. It felt like being caught in an ocean wave that was almost overwhelming me. Eventually, the water began to settle.

In that moment, I realized: *Wait a minute, this isn't personal. This is just a call for love from him.* I understood that I had a choice in how I saw the situation. I could continue seeing Christian as the problem, or I could shift my perception and choose to see him through the lens of love. And guess what? Just like that, the hurt I felt started to dissolve. When he came back into the kitchen, I said, "Hey, funny thing, I was just thinking that you're my problem... but I realized you're not!" I was laughing, truly laughing, at how my mind had tried to twist the situation.

Christian looked at me, softened, and said, "Yeah, I've just been stressed with work. I'm sorry I lashed out." And that was it — no lingering resentment, no days of silent treatment on either side. Just a real, honest, loving moment between us. That's what a holy relationship looks like: the willingness to see beyond the ego's attacks and to respond with love.

Now, I'm not saying I'm perfect at this. I still have my moments just like everyone else. But I know from experience that choosing to see each other through the eyes of love is the secret sauce that keeps a relationship alive and thriving. The alternative — the special relationship way — would have been for me to hold onto my anger, keep on making Christian wrong, and prolong the argument for days. And isn't that how most relationships end? Because we get stuck in our need to be right, in our need to make the other person the villain?

This, my friends, is serious stuff. Relationships are our greatest teachers. They show us all the places where we've forgotten who we are, where we've abandoned our own happiness. When we're willing to see things differently and stop blaming, we can start choosing love.

Healing Begins Within: Your Inner Relationship

If there's one thing I've learned in this wild, beautiful, and sometimes messy journey of spiritual growth, it's this: the only way to truly heal your relationships is to heal the relationship you have with yourself. It's usually not what we want to hear. It would be so much easier to blame our partner, our mother-in-law, or even the neighbor. But here's the thing if you want to change the way you relate to others, you've got to be willing to take a long, honest look in the mirror. Because, darling, that mirror is reflecting back all the parts of you that still need love, still need healing.

We live in this upside-down world where we believe that our happiness — or our misery — depends on what's happening out there. We think the issue is with our partner's bad mood, our friend's lack of understanding, or the impossible demands of our boss. But if you believe the problem is outside yourself, you lose. Why? Because you're giving away all your power to change the situation.

You see, the endless cycle of projections keeps our state of mind stuck in a holding pattern. We project our fears, insecurities, and judgments onto others, thinking that if they would just change, then we'd be happy. But all those projections are just a way to avoid dealing with what's really going on inside of us. It's like a game of emotional dodgeball, throwing blame at others so we don't have to feel the discomfort of our own stuff.

Taking Radical Responsibility

I've learned to heal my relationships with the uncompromising understanding that another person is not the cause of my upset. It doesn't matter what's happening or how intense the drama is. If I'm feeling hurt, angry, or disappointed, I've learned to ask myself, "What am I thinking and believing right now that's causing this suffering?"

And let me tell you, this isn't easy! When the proverbial "stuff" hits the fan, the last thing I want to do is look inward. But this is where the real change happens. When I stop blaming others and start looking at my own thoughts and beliefs, I get to see that it's my own mind that's causing the upset. Not my husband, not my kid, not the cranky cashier at the supermarket — just me and my thoughts. And guess what? That means I get to change it. It lets everyone else off the hook and puts the power to heal right back in my hands.

Mirrors, Mirrors Everywhere

Think of every relationship as a mirror. What you see in the other person is really just a reflection of what's going on inside you. If you're constantly feeling criticized by your partner, it's time to ask yourself, *"How am I being critical of myself?"* If you feel like your friend is always abandoning you, ask, *"Where am I abandoning myself? How am I not showing up for me?"*

This perspective can be challenging because it forces us to see that our happiness or lack thereof is not up to anyone else. It's always an inside job. That can be tough to swallow, but it's also incredibly liberating. It means that we don't have to wait for someone else to change to feel better. We can change how we see the situation, how we perceive the other person, and in doing so, we transform our entire experience.

Channeling Divine Guidance for Healing Relationships

This practice will help you tap into the wisdom within, giving you clarity on how to see your relationships with everyone including yourself, through the eyes of love. This is where healing begins: by turning inward and trusting the answers that come. This simple exercise will not only help heal your relationships but also strengthen your channeling muscles. Have a journal handy.

1. *Start with Yourself*

First, ask for guidance on healing your relationship with yourself. Find a quiet space and take a deep breath. Close your eyes and center your mind. Ask your Inner Wisdom: *"What do I need to know about healing my relationship with myself? What is the truth about who I am, and how can I experience more love within?"* Take a moment to listen. Journal and write whatever comes to mind. It may be a word, a feeling, or even a question that you need to explore more. Trust the process.

2. *Now, Ask About Your Relationships with Others*

Once you've reflected on your relationship with yourself, let's take it a step further. Now ask the Holy Spirit: *"What do I need to know about healing my relationships with others? What is standing in the way of love and connection?"* Again, write freely and allow whatever comes up to flow through your pen. It might be a shift in perspective, a feeling of compassion, or even a call to forgive. Trust that this message is for you.

The more you practice channeling your own answers, the clearer and more powerful the messages will become. Don't rush the process. Take your time and really feel into the answers you receive and trust the guidance that comes. Feel free to modify the questions. Stop reading here, take a stretch, and try this now if you can!

You're Doing the Work, and That Is No Small Thing!

If you've made it this far, let me just say: You're doing the work, and that is no small thing! Healing through relationships is one of the most challenging and rewarding journeys we can embark on. It's messy, it's raw, but it's also where the deepest transformations happen.

Remember, the goal isn't to get it perfect or never feel triggered again. It's about shifting your perspective, one moment at a time, and learning to see every relationship — whether it feels like a blessing or a burden — as an opportunity for growth and healing.

You've been willing to look at the hard stuff, to question the thoughts that have kept you stuck, and to invite love back into your perception. That willingness is your superpower. It's what turns every hurt into an opportunity for healing and every relationship into a doorway back to love.

So, keep showing up, keep choosing love, and keep being kind to yourself when you stumble — because stumbling is part of the dance. As you continue this journey, let your relationships be a reminder that you are never alone in this process. The Holy Spirit, the Divine, is always there, ready to guide you back to the truth of who you are.

You've got this, my friend. Now go out there, embrace the lessons, and let love lead the way.

You Are Present and Joyful

"Realize deeply that the present moment is all you ever have. Make the Now the primary focus of your life." — ECKHART TOLLE

I'M USING A QUOTE from Eckhart Tolle to start this chapter because his teachings on presence beautifully align with what *A Course in Miracles* encourages us to experience. He often speaks about making the "Now" our primary focus, stepping away from the constant mental chatter that keeps us distracted and away from peace. This is exactly what the Course aims to teach us through its lessons — to bring our attention back to the present moment, the "holy instant," where we can experience true peace and connection with the Divine. This instant is the only time there is.

When we fully embrace presence, we're aligning ourselves with our true nature — the part of us that is connected to God, to peace, and to joy. Let's dive into how living in the present can transform your life and help you live your happiest.

The Holy Instant: A Moment Beyond Time

In *A Course in Miracles*, experiencing the "holy instant" is central to knowing true peace and the presence of love. But what is the holy instant exactly? Think of it as a moment when you step out of the timeline, out of the past and the future, and fully embrace the now. It's like pressing Pause on all the stories, all the judgments, and all the worries that usually fill our minds. In that brief pause, you can experience a glimpse of eternity, a connection to your true Self beyond the illusions of this world.

The Course describes the holy instant as a moment when we choose to release the grievances and fears that keep us stuck in the past or anxiously anticipating the future. It's a moment when we let go of the ego's constant chatter and become fully present, allowing the mind to be quiet. It is in that quietness that we can hear the Voice of the Holy Spirit guiding us back to love.

ACIM teaches that the holy instant is also where true forgiveness happens. It's in this sacred moment that we can see beyond appearances, beyond our judgments, and glimpse the truth of who we are: perfect, whole, and free. In the holy instant, we remember that time is just an illusion, and that the eternal love of God is available to us right now, in this very moment.

This isn't about trying to force yourself to stay in the present, but rather allowing yourself to experience a moment free of judgment and full of grace. It's a surrender to what really is, a willingness to be guided back to the peace that is already within you. And the holy instant is always available to us, no matter where we are or what we're going through. It's like a doorway that's always open, inviting us back to the present where peace resides.

The Ego vs. the Holy Instant

The holy instant is a moment of pure presence, but getting there is an interesting journey, to say the least. The ego, our ever-present trickster, is determined to keep us tangled up in thoughts of the past or worries about the future. It thrives on these distractions because they keep us from the present, where we can access the peace that lies beneath.

The ego's main job is to convince us that the past holds all the answers to our pain or that the future will deliver what we lack. It whispers things like, "Remember how they hurt you?" or "What if this goes wrong?"— and just like that, we're pulled out of the present and into a loop of suffering. The Course teaches us that these thoughts are nothing more than illusions, but they can feel so real when we're in the thick of them.

Take my client Samantha. She came to me because she felt like she couldn't escape her thoughts — they were constantly dragging her back to painful memories of a breakup that happened years ago. She'd find herself replaying conversations, analyzing where things went wrong, and imagining different outcomes. Even though the relationship was long over her mind had kept her trapped in that past, unable to move forward.

One day, Samantha called me after a particularly rough day. She had run into her ex unexpectedly, and just seeing him brought a flood of emotions that she thought she had moved past. "It's like I'm back to square one," she said, her voice shaking. "I thought I had healed from this, but seeing him brought it all back."

I asked her to take a deep breath and notice where her mind had gone. "What are you believing right now?" I asked her. After a pause, she replied, "I'm believing that I'll never find someone like him again, that I'm unlovable, and that I missed my chance."

We took these thoughts into a deeper inquiry. "Is it true, Samantha?" I asked. "Is it absolutely true that you'll never find someone like him again? Is it true that you're unlovable?"

At first, she was convinced all that was true. But as she sat with the questions, a shift began to happen. She realized that these thoughts weren't facts; they were just stories her mind had created and stuck with. After Samantha sat with her thoughts, I asked her: "And most importantly, Samantha, how do you not know that him

YOU ARE PRESENT AND JOYFUL 79

not being in your life isn't the best thing ever? What is happening is the best because it's what's happening. When you deny that, you fight reality, and you lose your true nature." These stories were dragging her back into the past and keeping her from seeing new possibilities in the present moment.

I invited Samantha to consider the holy instant as a moment where she could let go of those stories and just be with whatever was true right now. We sat together and I guided her to breathe, place her hand on her heart, and let go of all the hurtful thoughts, even if just for a moment. I asked her to see the thoughts as clouds drifting by, knowing she didn't have to attach to them.

She took a deep breath, and I could hear the shift in her voice as she spoke. "In this moment, I'm okay," she said. "Right now, I'm safe. And I'm not that old version of myself anymore."

Samantha realized that the pain wasn't coming from seeing her ex; it was coming from her thoughts about what that encounter meant. In a holy instant, she could see her thoughts for what they were: just thoughts, not the truth. She began to understand that every time she let the past pull her out of the present, she was choosing to stay stuck in her suffering. But in the present, she had the power to choose differently.

Samantha's journey forward wasn't about erasing the memory of her ex or pretending that the past didn't happen; it was about choosing to stop letting those thoughts define her present reality.

The holy instant is a recurring practice, not a one-time fix. It's about recognizing when the ego is dragging us out of the present and gently guiding ourselves back. When we do, we get a taste of the freedom that comes from choosing love over fear, presence over projection. Boom!

The Link Between Presence and Joy

There's a reason why being present is so often associated with joy. When we're truly in the moment, we're no longer weighed down by the regrets of the past or the anxieties of the future. We're free to experience life as it unfolds — each breath, each sound, each sensation — without the layers of mental chatter that usually cloud our experience.

A Course in Miracles teaches that joy is our natural state, but it's a state we often forget because our minds are elsewhere. We think joy is something we need to find outside of us — something that will arrive when we get the promotion, when the relationship works out, or when we lose those extra pounds. But the Course and so many other spiritual teachings remind us that joy is always right here, right now, if we're willing to tune into it.

Think about a time when you've felt truly joyful. Maybe it was watching a sunset, laughing with a friend, or

YOU ARE PRESENT AND JOYFUL **81**

playing with a child. Chances are, during those moments, you weren't thinking about your to-do list or replaying a painful conversation in your head. You were simply present, fully immersed in the moment. That's the secret: joy is a byproduct of presence.

The ego likes to hijack our attention, pulling us into endless loops of "what if" and "if only." It tells us that we'll be happy when this or that happens, but it never lets us actually experience the joy that's available right now. The holy instant, as ACIM calls it, is our chance to see through the ego's lies and embrace the present moment.

Here's a practical example: One of my clients, Alex, struggled with constant anxiety about the future. He was always worrying about what might go wrong — whether he'd keep his job, whether his partner would leave, whether he'd ever have the life he dreamed of. Even when things were going well, he couldn't fully enjoy them because his mind was always racing ahead to the next potential problem.

We started working with the concept of presence, focusing on simple practices like bringing his awareness to his breath or noticing the sensations in his body whenever his thoughts started to spiral. At first, it was hard for him — he felt like his mind was constantly dragging him back into anxiety. But gradually, he began to experience moments of real peace, even joy, when he could stay present.

One day Alex called me excited to share an experience. He'd gone for a walk in the park, something he'd done a thousand times before, but this time he decided to really practice being present. He noticed the feel of the breeze on his skin, the sound of the leaves rustling, the warmth of the sun. And he felt a wave of joy wash over him — pure, unfiltered joy. He realized that nothing had changed in his external world, but everything had changed in how he was experiencing it.

He said to me, "Maria, it was like I'd been walking through that park my whole life but had never actually seen it before. And in that moment, I got it. I got what you meant about joy being in the present moment."

Alex's story is a reminder that joy doesn't come from controlling our external circumstances; it comes from how we choose to see the moment we're in. When we stop letting the ego's fears about the future and regrets about the past dominate our thoughts, we open up a space where joy can naturally arise.

It's not about forcing ourselves to be happy all the time or pretending that difficult emotions don't exist. It's about creating enough presence in our lives to experience the joy that's always there, beneath the noise and difficulties. It's about choosing to give ourselves the gift of the present moment, over and over again, even when it feels challenging.

The Course says, *"now is the closest approximation of eternity that this world offers."* (ACIM T-13.IV.7:5) When we understand that, we start to see the incredible power of the present. It becomes a portal not only to peace, but to the deep, abiding joy that is our birthright. Every time we choose presence, every time we return to the holy instant, we reconnect with that joy and remember that it's been with us all along.

A Guided Meditation for Experiencing the Holy Instant

Alright, my friend, let's dive into a simple but powerful practice* that will help you experience the holy instant for yourself. This is something you can come back to whenever you feel your mind wandering into the past or future, whenever you feel the pull of fear, whenever you just need a reminder of the peace that lives within you. It doesn't take long, but the results can be truly transformative. Find a quiet spot, get comfortable, and let's begin.

You can easily record this on your phone with your own voice to make it a personal practice, or if you'd like to be guided through this meditation by me, you can download it for free on my website:

www.mariafelipe.org *Just head over, grab your copy, and let's journey into the holy instant together.*

STEP 1: **Set the Intention**

Close your eyes and take a deep breath in

through your nose, then exhale slowly through your mouth. Do this a few times, letting your shoulders relax and your body sink into the space around you. As you settle in, silently say to yourself: I am willing to experience the holy instant. I am willing to let go of all thoughts and enter this moment fully.

STEP 2: **Grounding to the Present**

Bring your awareness to your breath. Notice the gentle rise and fall of your chest, the cool air as it enters your nostrils, and the warmth as it leaves. Let each breath remind you that right now, in this moment, you are safe. You are here. You are whole. If your mind begins to wander, gently guide it back to the breath. Imagine each thought that arises as a cloud drifting across the sky of your mind. You don't need to chase after the clouds or push them away; just let them pass by as you keep your focus on your breath.

STEP 3: **Connect with the Heart**

Now, place one hand over your heart and take a few more deep breaths, feeling the warmth of your hand against your chest. Imagine that with each inhale, you are drawing in light: a warm, golden light that fills your heart and spreads throughout

YOU ARE PRESENT AND JOYFUL **85**

your body. Feel this light filling you up, bringing a sense of peace and stillness to every cell. Silently repeat: *"This instant is the only time there is."* Allow this truth to wash over you. Let go of any need to control the moment and simply rest in the experience of being right here, right now.

STEP 4: **Release and Let Go**

Now, bring to mind a thought or worry that's been weighing you down. It could be something from the past or a fear about the future. As you hold this thought in your awareness, imagine offering it up to the light within your heart. See it being carried away on a gentle breeze, leaving your mind clear and open. Ask your Inner Teacher, the Holy Spirit: "Help me to see this differently. Show me the truth beyond this thought." Then, let go and allow yourself to rest in the quiet space that remains.

STEP 5: **Rest in the Holy Instant**

In this space of stillness, notice how the mind begins to quiet. Feel the peace that starts to emerge when you let go of thoughts about the past and future. It's okay if you don't feel anything profound right away — just know that in this moment, you are practicing presence, and that is enough. Allow yourself to rest here for a few minutes. If thoughts arise, gently return your focus to your breath and to the light in your heart. Trust that in this holy instant, you are connecting with your true nature — beyond all stories, beyond all illusions.

Step 6: **Gently Return**

When you're ready, take a few more deep breaths. Wiggle your fingers and toes, and slowly bring your awareness back to the room. Silently say to yourself: *"I carry the holy instant with me wherever I go. The present moment is my refuge, and I am never separate from the love that I am."* Open your eyes when you're ready, and give yourself a moment to appreciate this time you've taken for yourself. You've just created space for the holy instant, a space where you can return whenever the ego's chatter gets too loud.

Embrace the Now — Your Joy Awaits

If you've made it this far, let me just say: Your big willlilgness is making me do the happy dance! The practice of presence, the holy instant, and choosing to see beyond the ego's tricks isn't always easy, but it is so worth it. You are worthy of being in the present moment where all

YOU ARE PRESENT AND JOYFUL

happiness resides. You are worthy of living free from the constant pull of past regrets and future worries.

Remember, when you're not caught up in the stories of the past or anxieties about the future, you are in this happy instant where you can be free. It's a place where peace meets joy, where you can breathe fully, and where you can reconnect with the truth of who you are — beyond all the roles, the labels, and the noise.

And know this: each time you choose the holy instant, each time you choose presence over projection, you're not just changing your experience of this moment — you're changing your life. You are giving yourself the gift of true freedom, the kind that cannot be taken away by anything outside of you.

So, go ahead, my friend. Embrace the now. Let joy become your compass, and let the present moment remind you that you are already enough, already whole, already worthy of all the love and happiness you seek. This is your moment. Take it. Live it. Love it.

You Are Not a Victim

"I am not a victim of the world I see."
— ACIM Workbook Lesson 31

As we discovered in the last chapter, living in the present moment allows us to experience the joy and peace that are always available to us. When we let go of past regrets and future worries, we create space for the holy instant, where true happiness resides. But what happens when the ego pulls us into victimhood — that is, when we believe that life is happening *to* us, that we are powerless in the face of circumstances? That's what we're going to explore now. And let me tell ya, this has everything to do with living our happy!

From the moment we enter this world, most of us are taught to see ourselves as victims of unavoidable circumstances. Whether it's being hurt by someone else's actions, feeling trapped by a difficult situation, or simply believing that life is happening to us rather than for us, it's all too easy to slip into a victim mindset. But the truth, as ACIM teaches us, is that we are never truly victims. We are powerful creators, constantly choosing how to perceive and respond to the world around us.

When I did not know what I know now, I would play the victim. I blamed others for my pain, believing that if only they would change or behave differently, then I'd finally be happy. Whether it was in relationships, work situations, or even just the small annoyances of daily life, I was convinced that the problem was 'out there' and that I was powerless to fix it. But as I deepened my spiritual journey, I realized that this belief was keeping me *mucho* sad.

The Course is so empowering! It teaches us that the world we see is simply a reflection of our thoughts. It's not external events or other people that cause our suffering; it's how we think about and interpret them. Have I hit you over the head with this enough yet?? When we see ourselves as victims, we give away our power. But when we realize that we're the ones creating our experience through our perception, we reclaim that power and can choose a different way of seeing.

Novelas: *The "Victim" Dramas We Star In*

Let's talk about *novelas* — the soap operas we star in when we dive headfirst into the victim mindset. You know, the kind where we're the main character in a drama so

YOU ARE NOT A VICTIM **91**

intense even *telenovela* writers would be jealous. The over-the-top plots? Oh, we've got them. The endless "Why me?" scripts? Yup, those too.

One of my clients, Carolina, had her own *novela* moment recently. She was driving to meet a friend when, out of nowhere, she hit *la madre de todos los potholes*. Boom! Her car jolted, her coffee spilled, and she was sure her tire was flat. In a split second, her thoughts spiraled: "Why does this always happen to me? Am I cursed? Of course, the universe just loves making my life harder!"

In her *novela* storyline, this single pothole wasn't just an unfortunate bump in the road. Nope. It was evidence that life itself had it out for her. She wasn't just unlucky — she was *tragically doomed*.

But here's the thing about our *novelas*: they drain us. They pull us into overblown dramas where we forget the simple truth: we're not just the stars of the story, we're also the writers. Carolina's pothole wasn't a curse or a cosmic conspiracy; it was just... a pothole. When she stepped back, took a breath, and chose to rewrite her script, the drama disappeared, and she could laugh about it.

So next time you catch yourself starring in your own victim *novela*, pause and remember: *tú escribes el guión, meaning: YOU write the script.* You can choose to step out of the drama and into peace. Now, isn't that a plot twist worth watching?

Breaking Free from the Victim Illusion

A Course in Miracles teaches that the ego loves to weave a story in which we're powerless, trapped, and at the mercy of the world around us. It whispers that our happiness is entirely dependent on life going our way. But the Course invites us to see this for what it is: an illusion. The ego's victim narrative is a clever distraction from the truth of our power.

The lesson *"I am not the victim of the world I see"* offers a way out of this mindset. It teaches us that it's not the world or circumstances causing our pain — it's our thoughts about them. When we pause, take a breath, and question those thoughts, something miraculous happens. The thought itself begins to loosen its grip. And just like that, you're no longer a victim, my friend.

"The secret of salvation is but this: that you are doing this unto yourself." (ACIM T-27.VIII.10:1) While this might sound heavy at first, it's actually freeing. If the source of our suffering is within us, so is the power to let it go.

When we get our mind straight and see through the ego's lies, peace sneaks back in like it never left. The victim storyline? Gone. The ego? Probably sulking in the corner like a kid who just got caught stealing cookies. And there you are, remembering who you really are: a limitless, powerful, divine being who doesn't need to star in any more victim *novelas*. So next time the victim narrative tries to audition for a role in your life, just pause, question the

YOU ARE NOT A VICTIM **93**

thought, and let it know: *Sorry, this show's been canceled.*

The Illusion of Separation

One of the most profound teachings of *A Course in Miracles* is that the world we see isn't real — it's a projection of our mind. Yep, we've basically been watching the same old rerun of a movie we wrote, directed, and forgot we were starring in. The root of all suffering lies in identifying with this illusion, which the Course calls the "tiny, mad idea" (ACIM T-27.VIII.6:2). This is the idea that we could somehow be separate from God, separate from love, and separate from one another in a world we made up.

This "mad idea" gave birth to the ego, which is constantly on edge, trying to protect its fragile identity. The ego has one strategy: project, blame, and repeat. It whispers, *"It's not you, it's them,"* convincing us that our pain comes from external forces beyond our control. The ego thrives on conflict, turning every moment into a battle and every thought into evidence that we're powerless. No wonder we feel like victims — it's the ego's favorite trick.

But here's the good news: this entire storyline is based on a lie. As the Course teaches: *"What you see reflects your thinking. And your thinking but reflects your choice of what you want to see."* (ACIM T-21.in.1:2) In other words, if we're seeing a world of conflict, it's because we've been unknowingly handing the pen to the ego and letting it write our script. The truth is, we always have the power to choose again.

The Course calls us to wake up from this dream of separation and remember the truth: we are never disconnected from God, love, or one another. Beneath all the illusions, we are still as God created us: whole, innocent, and perfectly safe. The idea of separation may feel real, but it's just that — a feeling, not a fact. When we stop buying into the ego's fear and start questioning it, we open ourselves to an entirely different experience: one of connection, peace, and joy.

So, the next time the ego starts its usual drama about how the world's out to get you, take a deep breath and remind yourself: "I'm still in charge of this story, and today, I choose love instead of fear." Trust me, the rewrite is worth it!

Releasing the Victim Mentality

Can we really release the victim mentality? *A Course in Miracles* says yes — and it starts with the simple realization that we're not powerless. The idea of victimhood is a clever illusion created by the ego to keep us stuck, making us believe the world happens *to* us, not *through* us. But this illusion only has as much power as we give it.

One of ACIM's most empowering teachings is: *"I am responsible for what I see"* (ACIM T-21.II.2:3). Now, don't worry — this doesn't mean you're to blame for every challenging experience. It simply means your thoughts and beliefs shape how you perceive the world. If we're willing to question those thoughts, we can start loosening the grip of victimhood. It's not always easy, but it is possible.

Take this in for a moment: if the victim mentality is just a story we've been telling ourselves, what happens when we stop repeating it? That coworker who always "makes your life miserable" is no longer a villain; they're just someone doing their thing. That long line at the grocery store? It's just a line, not a personal attack. By shifting our interpretation, the world softens, and suddenly, you're free.

So, can we really release the victim mentality? Absolutely. But it takes practice. It's about noticing when the ego is spinning its drama and gently choosing not to buy into it. The miracle is realizing that the power to change the story has been in your hands all along. You're not a victim — you're the creator. And that's the most empowering realization of all.

Now, *fist pump*! Yeah!

Our Guide to Freedom from Victimization

In *A Course in Miracles*, the Holy Spirit is introduced as our Inner Teacher, the Voice for God, and the bridge that leads us back to the awareness of our true nature. While the ego loves to keep us stuck in fear, separation, and the victim mindset, the Holy Spirit offers a way out.

It gently guides us toward clarity, peace, and empowerment — reminding us that victimization is just another illusion.

You've already met the Holy Spirit in earlier chapters, and by now, you might notice a pattern: the Holy Spirit is all about freeing us from the ego's tricks. Victimization is one of the ego's favorite tools, but the Holy Spirit offers a different voice — one that reminds us we are not powerless, we are not separate, and we are certainly not victims of the world we see. Instead, we are creators, with the power to rewrite the stories the ego has sold us.

But here's the beautiful part: the Holy Spirit doesn't push or force us to change. It waits patiently for us to choose differently, respecting our free will every step of the way. The moment we get tired of the ego's drama and ask for help, the Holy Spirit steps in, offering us a fresh perspective. It shows us that the idea of victimhood is just a passing thought — not our reality.

As *A Course in Miracles* explains, *"The Holy Spirit is the highest communication medium. He abides in that part of your mind which is part of the Christ Mind."* (ACIM T-5.I.3:3) This means the Holy Spirit is already within us, waiting for us to tune in. While the ego shouts in chaos and confusion, the Holy Spirit speaks in calm, clear certainty. Its message is consistent: we are whole, we are safe, and we are deeply connected to God's love.

The Holy Spirit doesn't just teach us to let go of

victimhood — it shows us how to embrace our true identity as powerful, limitless beings. So, whenever you feel the pull of the ego's victim story, pause, breathe, and remember: you're not alone. The Holy Spirit is right there, ready to remind you, sweetheart: you ain't a victim — you're a victor!

How the Holy Spirit Guides Us Out of Victimization

Oye I know, when we're stuck in the victim mindset, it feels like the whole world is conspiring against us. Missed your morning coffee? *The universe hates you.* Stubbed your toe? *Clearly an attack.* But the Holy Spirit doesn't see things that way, thank goodness.

The Holy Spirit, our ever-patient inner guide, doesn't indulge in these dramatic storylines. Instead, it whispers, "Sweetheart, maybe it's time to step off the stage." While the ego thrives on keeping us in endless reruns of *The World Is Out to Get Me*, the Holy Spirit invites us to cancel the show altogether as we are learning here...

So, how does the Holy Spirit actually help us escape this exhausting cycle?

1. Spotting the Ego's Shenanigans:

The Holy Spirit has an impeccable radar for the ego's nonsense. When we're spiraling into victim mode, it doesn't join the pity party. Instead, it calmly points out that we've been buying into a story that isn't real. Think of it as your friend who kindly takes the wine glass out of your hand when you're mid-rant.

2. Turning Drama into Comedy:

The Holy Spirit knows how to inject a little humor into our crises. It gently nudges us to see the ridiculousness of the ego's over-the-top stories. Like, is forgetting your keys really proof that the universe is plotting against you? Maybe, just maybe, you could laugh and move on.

3. Reminding Us Who's Really in Charge:

Here's the truth: the Holy Spirit doesn't fix things for us. It reminds us that we don't need fixing. It quietly hands us the keys and says, "You've got this." Suddenly, you remember that you're the one who decides whether the day is ruined or if it's just a quirky story to laugh about later.

4. Letting Us Off the Hook:

One of the Holy Spirit's greatest gifts? Compassion. When we're tangled up in self-blame, it doesn't scold us. Instead, it says, "Hey, it's okay. You're learning." It turns out, you're not a victim — you're just human. And that's not so bad.

So, next time the ego tries to recruit you for another round of *Poor Me*, take a beat. Imagine the Holy Spirit giving you a wink and reminding you that life doesn't have to be so serious. You're not here to suffer — you're here to enjoy the ride. Take a deep breath, grab your sense of humor, and go show that ego who's boss. *Dale!* That is, LET'S GO!

Reflection:
Turning Drama into Divine Direction

As we've explored in this chapter, the victim mentality is just the ego's way of keeping us distracted and small. It thrives on drama and loves to keep us playing the same tired role. But here's the truth: you're not a victim — you're a creator. With the Holy Spirit as your guide, you have everything you need to step out of the ego's storyline and into one of empowerment and freedom.

The Holy Spirit doesn't ask for perfection, just willingness. It's not about fixing the world around you; it's about remembering the truth of who you are: whole, limitless, and deeply connected to divine love. This isn't a one-time deal — it's a daily practice, a moment-to-moment decision to choose freedom over fear, empowerment over blame, and joy over chaos. And guess what? You don't have to do it alone. The Holy Spirit is always on call, ready to offer a gentle nudge or a full-on intervention if you ask.

Holy Spirit, Take the Wheel!

I trust that with everything we've explored in this chapter, you're finally ready to let Spirit take the wheel.

The wild, bumpy ride of the ego? It's over. Done. *Finito.* Now, you're riding with the Holy Spirit — smooth roads ahead, my friend. You are not a victim of the world you see. You are a powerful being, and you deserve to live free from victimhood. Do you know your birthright? Do you know your truth? It's happiness. That's it. No more room for the *novelas*, the drama, the *caca*, the BS, or the victimization. You are way better than that!

So say it with your full voice: ***No more victim, no more drama!***

You Live Without Suffering

"Pain is a wrong perspective. When it is experienced in any form, it is a proof of self-deception."
— ACIM T-27.VII.1

A COURSE IN MIRACLES is clear: suffering is a choice. It's not about consciously choosing pain or fault; suffering stems from the ego's hidden beliefs and decisions, keeping us stuck. The Course teaches that suffering is not inevitable or necessary for happiness. Instead, it's a construct of the ego, which thrives on separation, fear, and lack.

In this chapter, we'll explore how to overcome obstacles like loss and hardship by shifting our perspective. I'll share the juicy story of how Christian and I came together and a miraculous moment that took place during my book tour in Mexico — one that will blow your mind! It was a moment of divine timing, where I learned that happiness is always available to us, even in the toughest times.

We'll also explore practical ways to stay grounded in

peace and realize that happiness isn't something to chase, but our truth waiting to be remembered. Suffering is an illusion, and happiness is always within reach when we step back into our true nature.

Let's dive in and discover how we can make happiness our new normal, no matter the circumstances.

Can We Be Happy 24/7?

When I was doing press interviews for my first book, *Live Your Happy*, I remember one interviewer asking me, "Well, can we really be happy all the time?" Without hesitation, I found myself saying, "Yes!" I surprised even myself. But as soon as I said it, the words started to flow naturally, and it all made sense.

If it's considered "normal" to be suffering, to have anxiety, or to experience depression, why can't the opposite be just as possible? Why can't happiness be the default setting? Why can't peace be the baseline of our experience? Why can't we experience life flowing with ease as our normal state? What if happiness was normal, peace was normal, ease was normal? Instead, we've made fear normal. *No mas!*

What if we could all decide to play "Opposite Day" and shift our collective perception as humanity? Why can't we all be happy 24/7? Now, I'm not talking about the cheerleader kind of happiness, smiling and cheering all the time. It's a deeper kind of happiness that comes

YOU LIVE WITHOUT SUFFERING **103**

from inner peace. It's a happiness that's like love itself — unconditional and unwavering. It's our birthright.

So, why have we stepped out from under the happiness umbrella? It's because we fall asleep to love. We start buying into the *caca* thoughts: the ones that tell us we're separate, we're not enough, or we need something outside of us to be happy. We forget who we really are. But here's the good news: our happiness never actually goes away. It's always there, like the umbrella, waiting for us to step back under its shelter. And guess what? We get to remember again! We get to wake up from the illusions and return to our true nature, where happiness is always available.

So, can we consider, even just for a moment, that happiness could be our default state? That we could live in a state of joy and peace, 24/7? Why not?

Happiness Is Natural

A Course in Miracles teaches that happiness is our natural state: it's who we actually are. Suffering is not required; it's an illusion, a result of the ego's misperception. In its simplest terms, ACIM says that we are extensions of God, and therefore we are extensions of love. If we are love, then joy, peace, and happiness are our natural inheritance.

"God's Will for me is perfect happiness." (ACIM Workbook Lesson 101) This means that it's not just a possibility

to be happy — it's the divine intention.

So why do we suffer? As I mentioned earlier, the root of all suffering goes back to what ACIM calls the "tiny, mad idea" — the moment when the Son of God (that's us!) entertained the thought of separation from God. As the Course puts it, this was the moment when the Son of God "forgot to laugh." Instead of seeing separation as impossible and laughing it off, we took it seriously. That meant we began to *believe* in the illusion of separation — and the result was our dream world of pain, fear, and suffering.

Forgetting to laugh at the notion of separateness also meant that we forgot our oneness with God, our oneness with each other, and our true nature as beings of love and light. Within this deep amnesia, the ego was born — a voice that constantly reinforces the ideas of separation, fear, and lack. The ego convinces us that we are alone, vulnerable, and at the mercy of a chaotic world. Then it whispers that happiness can only be found in external things, and gives us the painful task of "seek and do not find." (ACIM T-12.IV)

The happy news is that we are actually still in the mind of God, dreaming a dream of separation. None of this is real; it's all a projection of the ego's thought system. In reality we have never left God, and we never could leave love. Happiness and love are our natural states because we are still as God created us: whole, perfect, and eternally loved.

The suffering we experience is the inevitable result of buying into the ego's lies and forgetting who we are. But no matter how lost we feel, no matter how deep in the dream we seem to be, happiness is always there waiting for us to wake up. We are still in the mind of God, and nothing we have ever dreamed can change the truth of who we are.

The Holy Spirit is always there to guide us back. It helps us undo the belief in separation, one thought at a time. It helps us remember that suffering is not our destiny; happiness is. The Course invites us to bring all illusions to the light of truth. As we do this, we begin waking up from the dream. We start to remember that we are still safe in the mind of God, and that our natural state is one of joy, peace, and love. Then we can choose to wake up, to laugh at the idea of separation, and to reclaim our birthright of perfect happiness.

The Happiest Ending: My Journey Through Suffering

In Chapter 1, I mentioned the story of how Christian and I met. Here it is in more detail, as it goes hand in hand with overcoming suffering and living your happiest life.

In my first book, *Live Your Happy*, I shared a lot about my insecurities and struggles in relationships, including my difficulties with my first marriage and the pain of divorce. I suffered deeply during that time. Approaching my forties, I struggled with finding a partner while having an intense desire to become a mother, yet there was no quality relationship in sight. This left me in a cycle of longing and suffering for quite some time. In my relationships, I found myself repeating the same patterns: creating connections that weren't working, attracting destructive relationships, and constantly trying to convince men to love me. It was exhausting.

But everything changed in 2017 after the book was published. A true miracle happened, and it shifted everything. That was when I met my husband, Christian, at a spiritual event called The Happy Dream Retreat. How fitting, right? We connected instantly, and I could feel something special. A psychic had once told me that I'd meet my twin flame, connected to my book, and that we were already communicating. I don't always put my trust in psychics, but this time, it felt right.

I remember seeing Christian from a distance at the retreat — he had his hair tied in a bun, and I instantly felt something. But as he came closer, I noticed that he looked much younger and a lot shorter than I had pictured "the twin flame" would look like, LOL. "No, this can't be him!" But something drew me toward him anyway.

Christian and I met in February 2017. *Live Your Happy* was launched in March and by April, we were engaged. We got married in May, and went on a book tour together in May and June. By July, at the ripe old age of forty, I was pregnant with our little miracle, Ari. Talk about a whirl-

YOU LIVE WITHOUT SUFFERING

wind romance! Sometimes when you wish for something, it manifests faster than you can imagine.

The point of this story is twofold. First, I was suffering so much from not finding a partner or being a mother, but I kept giving that problem over to Spirit, trusting that God's will would be done. Even though I longed for these things, I was willing to let go, trust God, and surrender. It wasn't until October of 2016, when I declared that I was ready for my "Flirty Forties" and open to whatever the Universe had in store for me, that things started to change. I truly let go.

This is a story of trust — allowing things to run their course. Even though getting together with Christian didn't make logical sense, it felt right, and I couldn't say no. I was taken by the feeling of knowing it was right, and then my suffering transformed into a big, beautiful miracle.

Now, Christian and I have been married for eight years, and we are the proud parents of a seven-year-old. I couldn't be living my happiest life without going through the suffering, deciding to trust, and ultimately giving it all over to Spirit — letting God lead the way. It's always about surrendering to God's will, even when we think we know best. Because truly, we don't know anything compared to the wisdom of Spirit.

108   MARIA FELIPE

Trust:
The Key to Embracing Life Without Suffering

How do we suffer less, especially when the world seems to be unraveling? Wars, catastrophic fires, children being trafficked, families losing their homes — the pain can feel unbearable. And what about the unimaginable personal losses, like the death of a precious child? How do we not crumble under such heartbreak? The truth is, you do the best you can. The key lies in shifting your perspective and trusting in something greater than the loss, greater than the chaos.

Letting go of judgment is essential to cultivating trust. When we judge a situation as "good" or "bad," we're deciding — based on limited information — whether it's in our favor or not. Trusting means releasing judgment and knowing that everything that happens is ultimately for our benefit, even if we can't see it right now.

Trust, according to *A Course in Miracles*, is not about just hoping things will work out or blindly putting faith in a future outcome; it's about recognizing that everything that happens is part of a greater divine plan. The Course teaches us that all things are gently planned by One whose only purpose is our good. When we trust in this divine orchestration, we step out of fear and suffering and into the flow of love and peace.

As the Course reminds us, "you do not know what anything is for" (ACIM W-25.3:4). The big events, the

YOU LIVE WITHOUT SUFFERING 109

tragedies, all the things that shake us to our core — they are all part of a larger plan, even if we can't yet understand it. Acceptance, in this context, becomes an act of love and trust in God, even when it feels impossible. The Course teaches that everything in this world, no matter how painful, can be seen as a classroom for learning to let go of suffering. It's not about avoiding the pain but about recognizing the bigger picture and choosing love and peace over fear.

Byron Katie responded to a question about her mother by saying, "She's great. She's dead." That level of consciousness — seeing beyond the appearance of loss, without any judgment at all — is truly profound. It's not easy, and I'm definitely not there yet, but the thought that we could reach that level of peace in the face of everything is something to strive for. That's the real deal right there.

Here's a story that changed me forever.

A Miracle in Mexico: Trusting Love Beyond Pain

I was on a book tour in Mexico for the Spanish version of my book *Live Your Happy*, called *Vive Feliz*. The room was packed, and the workshop was extraordinary, filled with individuals willing to learn. During the Q&A, a woman stood up and asked me bluntly, "How can I be happy when my son has died? He was a doctor, only twenty years old, with a bright future ahead. How can I be happy after that?"

In that moment, Spirit took over. I could see her love, her innocence, and her truth. I met her exactly where she was, without judgment. I acknowledged her pain, her victimization, her fear — all of it was valid. I loved her unconditionally in that moment. Holding her hand, I said, "Would your son want to see you suffering like this? Or would he want you to celebrate his life and trust that his path, his choice, was perfect for his awakening?" I reminded her, "We don't know what's best for someone else, but we do know that love doesn't ask others to stay just so we can feel okay. Love wants others to be exactly where they need to be."

She began to soften. I held her in my arms as tears streamed down her face. The entire room was crying. In that sacred moment, a miracle occurred. It wasn't just for her; it was for all of us. We were reminded that even in our deepest pain, there is a higher perspective, a love that holds everything.

Living without suffering doesn't mean you won't feel pain. It means trusting in the unseen, in a divine purpose beyond what we can understand. It means choosing love and allowing miracles to transform our perception of loss. Even when the shit hits the fan, there's a way to see things differently — and that makes all the difference.

In the face of the world's suffering, *A Course in Miracles* offers a path to see beyond the chaos and find peace. It teaches us that, even in the darkest times, we can find forgiveness and healing through the lens of love, and we can trust that everything is unfolding as it should — even when we can't see it. That, truly, is the miracle.

A Simple Practice to Let Go of Control: Building Trust Even in Life's Toughest Moments

Here's a simple practice to help you let go of control and build your trust muscle, even when facing the big, tough challenges in life.

1. *Identify a Situation You Want to Control:* Take a moment to think of a situation where you're feeling the urge to control the outcome. It could be something big like dealing with a loss, tragedy, or a challenging personal circumstance. Remember, you can't change the circumstances, but you can change your response to them. As you face this hard situation, you have the power to shift how you see it and how you choose to respond, embracing trust in the process even when it's tough.

2. *Notice the Need to Control:* Pay attention to what happens in your body and mind when you think about controlling this difficult situation. Maybe you feel tightness in your chest, a knot in your stomach, or your thoughts racing with "*what if*s." The need to control often comes from fear — fear that things won't go the way we want, or fear that we won't be okay if they don't. Recognize that wanting to control is often a response to avoid pain or discomfort. Acknowledging this can be the first step toward releasing the grip of control and allowing peace to find its way in.

3. *Shift to Trust:* Take a deep breath. As you exhale, say to yourself, "I am willing to let go of control. I am willing to trust that everything is unfolding for my highest good." Remind yourself that just because you cannot change the circumstances, it doesn't mean you have to make the pain or fear your reality. You can't change your circumstances, but you can change your mind about them. Visualize yourself loosening your grip — releasing your attachment to how things should be or how others should behave.

4. ***Hand It Over:*** Imagine handing the situation over to the Holy Spirit, as if you're giving it to a trusted guide who knows what's best. Say silently or out loud, *"Holy Spirit, help me let go of my need to control this. Help me to trust that*

whatever happens is exactly as it should be for my growth and peace." By surrendering control, you allow space for guidance, wisdom, and peace to come through. *Give it all over.* You are not alone... *"Spirit, wow — this is a big one, and I am hurting. Show me the way out of this. I want to see things with love. Spirit, take the lead. Let me return my mind to Oneness. Help me look at this world with love, to hold the high vibration, and not add judgment on top of judgment."*

5. ***Focus on the Present:*** Bring your awareness back to the present moment. Notice your breath, the sensations in your body, and your surroundings. Trust is about releasing the future and bringing your focus back to the now. Remind yourself, "I don't know what anything means, but I trust that everything is unfolding for my highest good. What is happening is for a reason, and somehow, in some way, it's supposed to be this way." The present moment is where peace resides, and it's in this space that you can find comfort, even when things feel uncertain. (See Chapter 6.)

6. ***Watch for the Shift:*** As you go about your day, notice any shifts that occur when you choose trust over control. Perhaps a conversation goes differently than expected but leads to a deeper

> connection. Maybe a project takes an unexpected turn, ultimately leading to something better than you planned. As you release control, you make space for Spirit to work miracles in your life. Even in the most difficult circumstances, you might find yourself less worked up by the news or not as deeply affected by challenging situations, discovering new ways of being that bring unexpected peace.

Embrace Your True Nature

Now that we've explored how to live a life with less suffering, the question is: Are you ready to put these teachings into practice every single day? No more excuses, no more exceptions, no more compromises. It's time for a spiritual glow-up, my friend. We're coming to the end of this book, but the transformation is just beginning. Are you feeling the shift yet? Are you feeling more connected to your true nature, that deeper sense of trust? Have you realized how deeply God loves you, how you are never alone, and that you don't have to follow your ego into the chaos of "cray cray"?

Don't let worldly events take away your peace. Allow yourself to begin seeing loss and tragedy differently. Be filled with wonder, not fear. Don't add hate to hate, or judgment to judgment. As a lightworker, you have the power to raise the collective consciousness, to raise your own

YOU LIVE WITHOUT SUFFERING 115

vibration, and to hold a space of peace even in the toughest times. This is how you suffer less, and how you help others suffer less. Making the world more real, more chaotic, more filled with fear doesn't help anyone. But making God and His plan more real, more present, in every moment — that's where true peace lives.

It's time to take all the insights, miracles, and "aha" moments we've shared and make them a lasting part of our daily lives. As you step into this new phase, remember: you have the power to release control, trust the process, and surrender to Spirit. You are capable of navigating life's challenges with peace and grace, knowing that everything is unfolding for your highest good. In the next phase of your life, let's ensure that this transformation isn't just a momentary high, but a permanent and powerful change. Let's create lasting transformation and make it your new normal.

You Create Lasting Change

*"The Holy Spirit needs a happy learner,
in whom His mission can be happily accomplished."*
— ACIM T-14.II.1:1

IN THIS CHAPTER, we're diving into the "how" of creating lasting transformation. It's one thing to have a breakthrough moment or experience a temporary shift, but it's another thing entirely to live those changes to the max and embody them in our daily lives.

The Happy Learner

In *A Course in Miracles*, the concept of "the happy learner" is key to understanding how to truly create lasting change. So, what exactly is a happy learner? Simply put, it's someone who is willing to learn with joy, curiosity, and openness rather than resistance and fear. Being a happy learner doesn't mean that everything is easy and breezy. It does mean approaching life's challenges with a sense of wonder and a willingness to see things differently.

The happy learner doesn't expect the journey to be free from difficulty, but instead embraces challenging moments as opportunities for growth. When we're willing to learn happily, we recognize that every challenge or setback can be used by the Holy Spirit for our awakening. Our ego wants us to see our mistakes and setbacks as failures, so that we can give up, feel guilty, or judge ourselves and others. The happy learner knows that every development is part of the process, and mistakes are simply opportunities to learn and correct ourselves.

Think about a time when you felt resistant to something you needed to learn. Maybe it was a life lesson about patience or forgiveness. When you resisted, it probably felt like a struggle, like you were fighting against yourself. But the moment you decided to be open — even if just a little — to the lesson that life was presenting, then everything changed. You felt a little lighter, more hopeful. That's what the happy learner experiences: a shift from fear to curiosity, and from resistance to openness.

The Holy Spirit needs a happy learner because the process of transformation requires us to be willing to receive new perspectives. That means seeing with love instead of judgment, forgiving instead of holding grudges, and choosing again when we miss the mark. The happy learner embraces the journey with joy and understands that it's not about perfection — it's about being willing to see things differently, again and again.

"*Trials are but lessons that you failed to learn presented once again, so where you made a faulty choice before, you can now make a better one, and thus escape all pain that what you chose before has brought to you.*" (ACIM T-31.VIII.3:1)

One of the most important aspects of being a happy learner is recognizing that mistakes do not define us. They are merely steps on the path to growth. Instead of striving for perfection, we allow ourselves to grow, forgive, and keep moving forward without self-condemnation. When we approach our lives as happy learners, we open ourselves to the infinite love and guidance of the Holy Spirit. That's how miracles unfold.

The Spiritual Olympics, Baby!

I've said this time and time again: The only way to experience lasting change is to make a deep commitment to it. And this is why I always say: *big willingness is key.* You have to want it. You have to want to change your perception, to forgive, to let go of the old *caca*, and question your habitual thoughts even when you don't feel like it. A deep, unyielding desire is what places us in the Spiritual Olympics — training day in and day out for love.

In the Spiritual Olympics, there's no room for half-assedness — excuse my language, but it's true. It requires us to be dedicated athletes of love, fully committed to showing up, even when it's uncomfortable, even when it's easier to just stay in bed, and even when every part of your ego says, "Nope, not today." It means deciding, right here and right now, that nothing is more important than your happiest life. You have to wake up every morning and remembering that today is for your highest good, because today you will reconnect with Spirit.

How do we train for the Spiritual Olympics? We start with practices that connect us to our true nature:

- Wake up to a morning routine that sets you up for greatness: meditate, pray, practice gratitude — anything that aligns you with love and joy.
- Go for a brisk walk and as you do, talk to Spirit. Have a conversation with that part of yourself that is always there with guidance and love.
- Add to a daily gratitude journal, because there's always something to be grateful for.
- Sit still and forgive *yourself.* Let go of judgments you've been holding against yourself.
- Let go of some issue you feel the need to control or manipulate. Trust that life unfolds perfectly when you allow it to.
- Make that phone call you've been putting off. Reach out to someone you love.
- Start or continue writing that book, create that podcast, do the thing that Spirit is nudging you toward.

YOU CREATE LASTING CHANGE 121

- Choose to be happy instead of right.
- Stop controlling and manipulating and let God run the show!

The key to these Spiritual Olympics is *movement.* Love is active, dynamic, and always reaching to express itself in the world. Sometimes, students of the Course can get confused and think, "Well, this world isn't real, so why bother?" And while it's true that the Course teaches this world is an illusion, it's also true that it appears very real to us. Are you reading these words right now? Are you holding this book in your hands? Seems real enough, doesn't it?

The point is not to pass judgment on our illusions. That means that while we find ourselves here, we do things in the world with conviction, but *without attachment to outcomes.* We recognize that our true identity is beyond all this — but still we show up, engage, and choose love in every moment. We use the world as a classroom for awakening, as a place to practice being love in action. The Spiritual Olympics is not about denying the world, but committing to being the highest, most loving version of ourselves. This worldly experience, though temporary, is a chance to bring light to every corner of the world that seems obscured by darkness.

Manifesting without Guilt

Now it's time to address something that's buzzing around everywhere: manifesting. I want to dive into what *A Course in Miracles* says (and doesn't say) about manifestation, because I know it's a topic that causes a lot of confusion. I've struggled with it myself as a Course student.

The way the world talks about manifesting can often leave us feeling like there's something outside of us that we have to grab to be happy. It's a constant chase for money, relationships, professional success, or some other external sign of "abundance." And it comes with a lot of greed, guilt, and endless searching. And that endless search brings us mostly greed and guilt.

So what does *A Course in Miracles* actually say about manifesting? How do we create good in the world, make things happen, and still stay aligned with our true purpose? How can we embrace our potential without always feeling that we need more, more, and more?

The Course doesn't ask us to give up our desires, or live a life devoid of things that bring us joy or fulfillment. Instead, the Course invites us to see our desires differently: as opportunities for learning. When we desire something, whether it's a better job, a relationship, or more abundance, the key is to recognize that these desires are not inherently bad or wrong.

But we do need to ask: What is the purpose behind these desires? Are we using them to reinforce our sense of lack and separation, believing that something "out there" will eventually, finally complete us? Or are we using them as an opportunity to grow closer to Spirit, to understand more deeply the truth of who we are? It all comes back to the purpose we give to what we want.

The Course teaches us that every situation, and every desire, can serve either the ego or Spirit. The ego's desires are always driven by a sense of lack: "I need this to be happy, and if I don't get it, I'm incomplete." The Holy Spirit reminds us that our deepest need is for inner peace and connection to love.

Manifestation as a Miracle

According to ACIM, a miracle is a shift in perception. It's the moment when we stop seeing our desires as something that will fix us and start seeing them as a doorway to healing. It's about shifting from *"I need this to feel worthy"* to *"I am already worthy, and if this desire unfolds in alignment with love, then wonderful. If not, I am still complete."*

We often think of manifesting in terms of the material world: more money, a new car, a dream vacation. And while there's nothing inherently wrong with any of these things, the Course teaches us that true manifesting is about allowing our mind to align with Spirit. When our mind is in alignment with love, outward circumstances tend to fall into place naturally. We become less attached to outcomes and more focused on the deepest feeling behind what we want. True Abundance is basically remembering that you are as God created you. That means recognizing that *what you have is what you want.* Reality is heaven. When we fight it, that's hell.

What if we approached manifestation as an extension of love rather than a way to fill a perceived gap? When we align our desires with the fundamental purpose of extending love, our whole relationship with manifesting changes. Instead of thinking *"I need this to be happy"* we can think *"How can I allow what I desire to be a vessel for love?"*

For example: Maybe you desire financial abundance. Instead of seeing it as a way to feel secure or powerful, you could see it as a way to bring more good into the world. You could ask yourself, *"How can I use a greater abundance to be a light to others?"* This shift in perspective gradually transforms the ego-driven desire for *more* into a generous expression of your true nature.

Enjoy the Play, But Don't Get Caught Up

The Course says we're dreaming the world, but that doesn't mean we can't enjoy it. Imagine you're in a play. While you're on stage, you get to enjoy your costume, the sets, and your role. But you know you're not actually the character; you're an actor playing a part. The Course encourages us to engage with life fully, to enjoy it, but not to mistake the character we're playing for our true Self.

Manifesting, creating, dealing with the daily world as we see it — all this is part of the play. We get to have fun with it, enjoy it, and see what unfolds. Ultimately, our happiness doesn't depend on what happens in the play. It comes from remembering that we are the eternal, unchanging Love that is behind it all.

Manifesting with Spirit: True Prayer

I'm excited to share with you my favorite way to manifest. For me, it's about setting goals with soul — aligning them with the Holy Spirit. This practice allows you to express all your desires without guilt or hesitation. Here's how you do it:

1. **Write it All Down:** Write down everything you desire — no filters, no holding back. Whether it's starting a podcast, making $5k a month, traveling the world, or something else — put it all on paper. This is about clarity and openness.

2. **Create Your Altar:** Envision an altar. Place everything you've written down on the altar, physically or mentally. If you like, wrap each desire in a small gift box to symbolize your offerings. This represents your willingness to receive what's in alignment with love.

3. **Invite the Holy Spirit In:** Ask the Holy Spirit

> to meet you at your altar. You are not alone in this. Hold the intention that these desires are not to be idolized, but given over to God's will.
> 4. **Surrender:** Say aloud: *"God, I give over these desires to You. I do not want to place any idols before You. I want what You want for me. May Your will be done."*

This process is pure gold — manifesting in alignment with your true nature. It's about trusting God's plan and stepping aside so the highest and best can enter. It has changed my life, the lives of many students, and I trust it will change yours too!

I must confess, this was one of the practices I leaned on when I deeply desired to be in a relationship, start a family, and become a mother. I made it a habit to surrender it all to Spirit. This "prayer practice" helped me trust and brought me a sense of peace. Then — just one year later — I met Christian, and soon after, I became pregnant with Ari.

Life is full of surprises! Gotta love it!

It's Okay to Be a Hot Mess

But let's be honest: because we're not free of ego and neither is anyone else, we will often feel that we haven't done our best. We want to act in love, and live out our best intentions, but we don't always follow through. And then we end up feeling guilty. Cultivating an uncompromising nature and following through on our promises requires allowing ourselves grace when we fail. It's okay to fall short. We're in a cuckoo world with cuckoo thoughts, and there are times when we just don't feel like we're living well. And that's okay.

Here's a story of when I personally was a hot mess shortly after giving birth to Ari. About three months postpartum, I made the not-so-intelligent decision to do a couple of book events, one of which was in Fort Lauderdale, FL. I was still navigating hormonal shifts and not feeling like myself. And here I was, driving to an event for my book *Live Your Happy* when, ironically, I wasn't feeling remotely happy.

Thankfully, angels have my back. When I arrived, the kind person running the event welcomed me with so much love. She led me to a beautiful room filled with crystals and the soothing scent of aromatherapy. Sensing how I was feeling, she looked me in the eyes and said, "Take your time. Come out whenever you're ready."

I sat with Spirit, fully surrendered, and gave myself permission to feel everything: the messiness, the exhaustion, the overwhelm. I chose to give the workshop completely over to Spirit. I embraced grace and let myself simply be.

When I finally stepped out, there were about twenty

people in the room. I closed my eyes, tuned into the energy, and then opened them to welcome everyone. The first thing I said was, "I'm about to give a talk on happiness, but honestly, I'm not feeling remotely happy right now. I actually feel like a hot mess. Anybody else feeling this way?"

To my surprise, most of the room raised their hands. That simple act of honesty set the tone for deep healing. Authenticity is where we meet each other in our truth. It's where we allow ourselves to be exactly as we are, without judgment.

What this story teaches us is that we don't need to put up a façade. We don't need to pretend. When we show up as our true selves, we teach others that they can do the same. We give them permission to embrace their own hot-mess moments. And that is powerful.

The ego will tell us we should feel guilty whenever we fail or fall short. But a guilt-free attitude is the key to living without compromise. If you get some needed exercise, great! If you don't, that's okay too. It's crucial to give ourselves grace, which often means not kicking ourselves when we're already down. Whatever comes up, just honor yourself, even if you're honoring your resistance. It's about loving yourself exactly where you are.

So it's okay to be a hot mess sometimes. It's okay to not want to get up from the couch. The key is to notice what you're doing, and notice the guilt you feel while you're sitting on that couch. That's where real freedom lies.

It's about ending the constant chant of *coulda, shoulda, woulda*. You have to be uncompromising not just about your highest aims, but also about living without guilt, shame, and judgment. Whatever you decide to do, let it come from love.

Living as a Happy Creator

As we wrap up this chapter, remember that you are a powerful creator. Not because you can control everything around you, but because you have the power to choose how you perceive the world. Our real power lies in our willingness to align with Spirit and allow our desires to serve love instead of fear.

We are here to learn, to grow, and to extend love. Our desires, our creations, and our dreams are all part of this learning. They are part of the journey that helps us remember who we really are: extensions of divine love. The key is not to deny our desires or feel guilty about them, but to let Spirit guide us, transforming even the smallest of our wishes into something that brings more light into the world.

Imagine what life could be like if we woke up each day ready to create, ready to share, ready to serve — knowing that every desire, every intention, every manifestation is an opportunity to remember our true nature. Imagine how powerful it could be if we truly lived with big willingness, allowing Spirit to guide us in every step we take.

So, as you go forward, I invite you to embrace the joy of being a happy learner, a happy creator, and a happy manifester. Know that you are never separate from the love that you are. Your happiness, your power, and your peace are always within you. And every time you align with Spirit, every time you choose to see things differently, you bring a little more heaven to this earth.

You Live Your Happiest

"God's will for me is perfect happiness."
—ACIM Workbook Lesson 101

CONGRATULATIONS — you've made it to the happiest place: this moment, right now. Welcome to Chapter 10!

As you've journeyed through this book, you've come to understand that believing our ego-driven thoughts is the ultimate cause of our suffering. And it's not even the thoughts themselves that are the issue, but our attachments to them. We believe the problems of this world are truly real. We also tend to believe that others are to blame, and in self-defense we compare, judge, and manipulate. But to be truly happy, we must begin to wake up. That means we must be willing to change our perceptions, no matter what it takes. (Unless, of course, you prefer to be unhappy. And that's okay too.)

What I do know from my own experience is that only love is real. No matter what we ultimately choose, happiness will eventually prevail because God holds that truth for us. We do have a loving Father — that is, a part of our minds that knows better than the ego — and since we are living here as humans in this dream, let's live it happier, lighter, and free. We know that is God's will for us.

The messages I've been teaching for a while now have resonated with many people. This is why I created a simple formula to integrate all these teachings into a practical, daily practice. Let's dive in!

The Live Your Happy Formula

The Live Your Happy Formula is the culmination of everything I've learned over 25+ years of studying, practicing, and sharing *A Course in Miracles*, including my own journey to happiness. Whether I'm guest speaking, leading a master class, or working one-on-one, this formula embodies the heart of everything I teach, distilled into a simple, three-step method that makes transformation accessible. This is not just a theory — it's a practical tool that you can use every day to redefine your experience and start living your happiest life.

Define It, Heal It, Live It
1. Define It

To create lasting change, the first thing we need to do is define our big problem. This means getting really clear

YOU LIVE YOUR HAPPIEST

133

about what's troubling you. Is it a particular feeling, situation, or an ongoing pattern? Identifying it is the key first step — bringing awareness to what's beneath the surface.

In this step, we take the time to look at what *appears* to be causing our suffering. As ACIM puts it, "*The world I see holds my fearful self-image in place, and guarantees its continuance. While I see the world as I see it now, truth cannot enter my awareness.*" (ACIM, W-56.3:2-3) To define our one big problem — that is, the errant way we've chosen to see the world — we have to shine a light into those hidden corners where discomfort or fear may be lurking. By getting honest about what we're really feeling, we can start to untangle the fundamental cause of our suffering.

This step can be difficult, especially if we're feeling stuck in a sense of victimization. When we're deep in suffering, it can be hard to see the root cause clearly. But that's why it's so important to just do your best: Lean into that big willingness to see our real problem. Sometimes, simply acknowledging that we are willing to try is enough to begin the process of change.

In this step, you start by identifying any thought that is causing you to feel upset. For example, you might say, "I am angry at _____ because of _____." You might be angry at the world or a particular person; the target doesn't matter. By putting your upset into words, you bring the underlying belief or thought to the surface. Often, just stating our upset plainly reveals a lot about what we are really dealing with.

You don't have to do this alone. In fact, it helps so much to look at it with your inner companion — whether you call it the Holy Spirit, your Higher Self, or your Inner Teacher. This step is about bringing what's troubling you into the light, and you have a powerful guide to help you see clearly. Invite that gentle, loving presence to help you define what's causing your upset.

Once you know what your specific upset is, it's time to take a different look at it. As I have mentioned again and again ACIM Workbook Lesson #5 suggests: *"I am never upset for the reason I think."* This means that our suffering is not caused by external events, but by the meanings we assign to them. Those meanings arise directly from our habitual thoughts and beliefs, which can be changed regardless of unpleasant events or difficult circumstances. In turn, that means that the source of our suffering — and ultimately our peace — lies within us.

So, to usefully define what's bothering us, we have to go beneath the surface of what seems to be happening "out there" and start to see the real root of the pain: our interpretation of the world around us. It's not about blaming or judging ourselves, but it is about having the courage to be truly honest with ourselves.

Take a moment to sit with yourself and ask, "What is really bothering me?" Allow yourself to look at whatever it is without trying to change it or make it wrong. Define what it is, where it comes from, and how it's showing up in your life. This act of defining is an act of self-awareness, a way to look clearly at the cause so we can move to the next step.

2. Heal It

Once you've defined what's troubling you, the next step is to heal it. This begins with making the commitment to see the situation differently. You can simply say, "I am willing to see this differently." This openness is where healing truly begins. Instead of blaming anyone, including yourself, for the situation, you challenge your interpretation and ask, "Is this really true?"

Take, for example, a thought of mine like "I'm sad because Christian is being mean and moody." Here, I can start to examine what how I'm interpreting his behavior. Is it true that his mood causes my sadness? Or is this just a story I'm telling myself to avoid looking inward for a deeper cause? This is when I invite the Holy Spirit to help guide this healing.

"If you knew Who walks beside you on the way that you have chosen, fear would be impossible." (ACIM T-18. III.3:2)

You aren't alone in this process. As we have learned, a miracle is simply a shift in perception, and this step is all about allowing that miracle to happen. As you access a deeper part of your mind, you begin to see that the beliefs and judgments that seemed so real are not fixed; they are just thoughts that can be transformed.

Remember, healing isn't about forcing positivity or ignoring your feelings. It's about acknowledging your emotions and understanding that they come from your thoughts, not the external world. As you go through this step, give yourself grace. Sometimes, the process of questioning our beliefs can be uncomfortable or even painful, but it's also the gateway to freedom. Each time you do this work, you are releasing layers of illusion and coming closer to the truth of who you really are.

Healing is the process of reclaiming your power. It's the choice to be free from the story that you are a victim of the world you see. You look at the thought that's causing your pain, question it, and open up to a new way of seeing (refer to Chapter 2 for help). Every time you do that, you take another step toward living your happiest, most authentic life.

3. Live It

The final step is to live it. This means integrating everything you've learned into your daily life, embodying these realizations so they become second nature. Living it means setting up practices that reinforce this new way of thinking and being. It's about creating a daily routine that supports your happiness — a life that aligns with the truth of who you are.

This step might be the most important one when it comes to creating lasting happiness. To truly live your happiest life, you need to embody and apply these insights consistently. This means practicing non-judgment daily, questioning your untrue thoughts, letting go of the need to control, and trusting in the divine flow of life. It means showing up authentically and honestly, not just with others but with yourself too.

Living it also means working on your relationships in a different way. You take responsibility for your part in them, letting go of the need to be right. It's about choosing to be happy rather than being right? *Comprende*? Instead of falling into old habits of blame and attack, you begin to approach every interaction with a sense of openness, willingness, love and big-time awareness.

You live your healing by taking every grievance, every fear, every doubt to the first two steps: define it and heal it. This is where being uncompromising comes into play. You are unapologetically committed to your happiness, which means that you refuse to let grievances, judgments, or fear take hold of your mind without bringing them to the light. It's not about perfection; it's about persistence. You make the decision to practice, and when you falter, you choose to start over.

Ultimately, this step is about creating a lifestyle that supports your happiness and freedom. That could mean starting your day with meditation, taking moments throughout the day to check in with your thoughts, or practicing forgiveness of just about everything you see on a daily basis. This is how transformation takes place and accelerates.

When you live it, you are not just changing your life — you are creating ripples of change that impact everyone around you. This is the power of living your happiest.

Example of the Formula in Action: Navigating Extreme Pain

Inspired by a story I shared in an earlier chapter, in which a woman lost her son and found herself devastated, let's use her experience as an example of how the *Live Your Happy* formula can be applied.

You are devastated by the passing of your son. The grief feels unbearable, and your thoughts repeat: "I can't go on. This loss is too much for me to bear."

Define It: Pause and acknowledge the pain you are feeling — grief, sorrow, devastation. Allow yourself the time to sit with it, to be open for change. Sit with yourself and your thoughts, and just know that you are not alone in starting this process of healing. Spirit has your back. Notice the thoughts that fuel your pain: *"I've lost a piece of my heart"* ... *"Life will never be the same"* ... *"I'll never be happy again."* By recognizing these thoughts as stories you're telling yourself, you can begin to see that while the grief is real, much of it is magnified by the beliefs you hold

YOU LIVE YOUR HAPPIEST **139**

about what this loss means. The thoughts themselves are where the suffering begins. Say to yourself: "I am open and willing to see this differently."

Heal It: Now, challenge these thoughts. Ask yourself, "Do I know for certain that I can't go on? Is it true that life can never hold joy again?"

Take it a step further — be radical. Is my son really dead? Can he only be a body? Reflect on the truth that *"I am not a body, I am free."* (ACIM Workbook Lesson 199) His essence is alive in spirit, just as yours is. Ask yourself: "How do I *not* know that this is not the best thing for him, for me, for the greater plan? Maybe he is saving himself from future suffering, or helping to unfold a larger purpose that I cannot yet see."

Shift your perspective: "What if I allowed myself to feel this pain fully, without resistance, trusting that healing is possible, no matter how distant it feels right now?" Affirm: "I am willing to see this differently. Though this loss feels overwhelming, I can choose to trust that something greater is unfolding. I love him, and that means allowing him to be where his soul has chosen to be. His spirit remains, and with that love, I can move forward, knowing that his essence is eternal and untouched by death."

Live It: Begin to live from this new perception, taking small steps forward. Light a candle in your son's honor, speak to his spirit, and express your love and longing. Let yourself cry, but also remind yourself: *"His essence* *remains with me in love.*" Allow the grief to be what it is without the need to change it immediately. Seek support from friends, family, or a spiritual practice, and honor your process. Commit to small acts of self-care, knowing that healing is gradual, unfolding with each moment. Repeat: *"I choose to move forward, step by step, guided by love."*

The journey through deep grief is not about forcing the pain away, but about allowing yourself to feel it while trusting that healing can and will come, even if it's not clear how. It's through surrender and love that space for healing is created.

Live Your Happiest

I hope you finally got the memo: Happiness is your birthright. You are worthy of living a life that feels free, fulfilling, and deeply alive — *ahora, mañana y siempre!* I hope you'll take the *Live Your Happy* formula you've learned in this chapter and put it into practice as you continue your journey in this cuckoo world.

When I say "cuckoo," I'm acknowledging that this world often appears very real and very troubled. But we are not of this world. We are the light of the world, and our purpose here is to live in joy. Humor, laughter, and delight are attributes of our true nature, as they are reflections of the unconditional, loving Light within. As Byron Katie says, *"You are your own suffering, you are your own happiness."*

And as *A Course in Miracles* reminds us: *"Nothing real can be threatened. Nothing unreal exists. Herein lies the peace of God."*

The time has come to walk with a genuine, gentle smile — even when the *caca* is hitting the fan.

May this book be a practical guide you return to, and may it continue to bless you. You are so worthy of living a suffering-free life!

Thank you from the bottom of my heart for taking the time to read this book, for your big fat willingness to see the truth, and for having the courage to go all in on your happiness — no matter what it takes.

Now go out there and ***Live Your Happiest!***

If you have enjoyed *Live Your Happiest* and want to go deeper, Maria offers in-person events, online courses, coaching, and more to inspire your journey toward true happiness and inner peace. For information about all these offerings, and more, visit *www.mariafelipe.org.*

Newsletter

Get weekly inspirational emails with deep reflections to live happier, announcements, and first access to new resources. (Free)

7-Day True Happiness Challenge

A unique and radical challenge that helps you stop sabotaging your happiness and recognize your True Nature. You get a daily power talk, practice and daily challenge to keep your happy in check! (Free)

Happy Miracle Membership

A thriving community living the Course! Each month you'll receive a new workbook based on a theme, guided meditations, master classes, access to a monthly ACIM study group, and more.

1-on-1 Coaching

Personalized sessions with Maria to help you live your happiest and overcome challenges.

Programs

- *Healing the Inner Child:* A journey to nurture and heal your inner child for deeper peace.
- *Spiritual Awakening:* Tools and teachings to awaken your connection to Spirit.
- *9-Week Online Program:* Maria's most popular course, based on Live Your Happy, is a 9-week online experience that serves as a practical ACIM handbook. It's raw, real, and radical, guiding you to heal relationships, live with purpose, and apply powerful practices right away.

Live Workshops and Online Courses

Interactive programs designed to support healing, forgiveness, and empowerment inspired by *A Course in Miracles.*

WhatsApp Group: ACIM with Maria Felipe

Get weekly messages, inspiration, and practices to help you live *A Course in Miracles.* (Free)

Motivational Speaking

Uplifting talks that inspire audiences to live their happiest lives. With over a decade of speaking experience, Maria captivates and motivates audiences to embrace transformation & joy.

Maria's YouTube Channel

Discover talks, meditations, and much more to support your spiritual journey. (Free)

About the Author

A Cuban American born in Miami, Maria Felipe is a dynamic motivational speaker and author who is changing lives one laugh at a time. With a passion for inspiring others, she has become a sought-after speaker who motivates and encourages audiences with her unique blend of humor and wisdom.

Before becoming a spiritual teacher, she appeared in national commercials and hosted successful TV shows, including World Wrestling Entertainment shows with live audiences of twenty thousand. After experiencing an inward calling, she changed course and studied with Pathways of Light, an accredited school inspired by *A Course in Miracles*. With a warm and engaging style, Maria has helped countless individuals to overcome obstacles and live happier!

People magazine once referred to Maria Felipe as "*Una campeona sin rival*, or "a champion without rival."

Aside from her career, Maria loves being a mom and wife, and is grateful to be living in sunny Florida with her family. For more information on Maria's book's, workshop, programs and coaching visit her website or social media.

www.mariafelipe.org

Social Media

Facebook
www.https://facebook.com/mariafelipefanpage/

Instagram
www.instagram.com/a.course.in.miracles
www.instagram.com/revmariafelipe

Youtube
www.youtube.com/@MariaFelipe

Tiktok
www.tiktok.com/@acimwithmaria

X (Twitter)
www.x.com/RevMariaFelipe

Apple Podcast
https://podcasts.apple.com/us/podcast/maria-felipes-show/
id1242513531

Acknowledgments

As I sit down to write this section, my heart is filled with gratitude for the many souls who have walked this journey with me and made this book a reality. Each of you has been a divine blessing in my life, and I am forever grateful.

To my beloved son, Ari, you are my greatest teacher and my deepest joy. Your light reminds me daily of what truly matters, and your love fuels my soul in ways words cannot express.

To my husband, Christian, my #1 supporter, thank you for consistently encouraging me and guiding me to spread my message. Your unwavering belief in me has helped take my work to a whole new level. I'm especially grateful for the beautiful book cover you created—it is absolutely perfect and captures the essence of this book in a way I could never have imagined. Te amo mi amor.

To my assistant, Germán Chamorros, thank you for your incredible work in getting my voice out into the world through social media and for ensuring our community is always cared for. What a team we are—two souls running an empire!

To my community, clients, and followers, you inspire me every single day. Your love, support, and engagement fuel my passion to keep going and serve in meaningful ways.

To my literary agent and editor, D. Patrick Miller, thank you for your guidance throughout the writing process. for your guidance throughout the writing process. Your insights, patience, and expertise have been invaluable.

To Byron Katie and Stephen Mitchell, thank you for your gracious support and for allowing me to integrate 'The Work' into this book. Your kindness and wisdom have deeply touched my heart.

To my family — my dad, Pablo Sosa, my brother, Jesús Felipe, and my mother, cheering me on from the heavens — your love and encouragement has helped me become who I am today.

To my dear contributors — whose generosity through crowdfunding helped bring this book to life — thank you for believing in this project and supporting its creation.

To the teachings of *A Course in Miracles,* which have been a constant source of inspiration and guidance in my life. This book is a reflection of the miracles I have witnessed through its lessons.

To Spirit, for its loving guidance, thank you for the gifts of truth and inspiration that have flowed through you in this work. May it serve as a beacon of light for all who read it.

Finally, to you, the reader, thank you for opening your heart to this book. It is my hope that these words inspire and uplift you, guiding you closer to the peace and freedom that are your birthright.

With deepest gratitude,
Maria Felipe

148

Contributors

Ramon Silva

Kelly Reamer

Valerie Burke

Rev. Karol Scotta

Teresa LaMontagna

Patti-jo Lenox

Stacy Sully

Helena Hebibovic

Cynthia Ferguson

Jackie Lora Jones

Christine Johnson

Barbara Adams

Louise D'Allura

Celine Granato

Christian Mauerer

Madonna Murphy

Rev. Cathy Silva

Tom Vargas

Beth Lucas

Pablo Sosa

Micki Barreto

Deana Cheshier

Printed in Great Britain
by Amazon